- What tree has no leaves?
  - What tree would make one hundred small homes?
    - What wood burns brightly when green?
      - What bark is as lasting as rock?

A Pocket Guide to Trees is no dry recital of details and distinctions, but rather a parade of tree personalities.

It covers the trees of all parts of the United States including the great pines and cedars of the Northwest; the spectacular redwoods and eucalyptus trees of California; the strange mesquite, and blue palo verde of the southwestern deserts; the exotic palm and fruit trees of southern Florida, and many more across the country.

A Pocket Guide to Trees
was originally published by
Dodd, Mead & Company, Inc.

Other books by Rutherford Platt:

The River of Life
This Green World
1,001 Questions Answered About Trees
The Woods of Time (Original title: *Our Flowering World*)
Worlds of Nature

A POCKET GUIDE TO

TREES

BY RUTHERFORD PLATT

(Original title: *American Trees, A Book of Discovery*)

WITH DRAWINGS BY
Margaret L. Cosgrove

PHOTOGRAPHS BY THE AUTHOR

PUBLISHED BY POCKET BOOKS NEW YORK

A POCKET GUIDE TO TREES
(Original title: American Trees, A Book of Discovery)

Dodd, Mead edition published 1952

POCKET BOOK edition published May, 1953

7th printing.......................August, 1974

A Pocket Guide to Trees was previously published under the imprint of Washington Square Press, a division of Simon & Schuster, Inc.

L

Standard Book Number: 671-78807-8.

Printed in the U.S.A.

SOMETHING MARVELOUS IS GOING ON HERE!

Take any tree. Hang a sign on it announcing *"Something marvelous is going on here!"* Everybody who has the least sense of wonder will stop to find out what is going on.

Such a sign does hang on every tree—addressed to all the senses of sight, hearing, smell, taste, and touch.

Sometimes it is spectacular, and appears and disappears like a big electric sign in Times Square: the fall flaming of maple; the white foam of dogwood in the spring; cottonwood "snow" covering the ground; the roar of trees in a storm.

Sometimes the sign that "something marvelous is going on" has peculiar delight: the fragrance of balsam; the taste and crackle of a cold apple; the swirling patterns and rich colors in the wood of fine furniture.

Again, trees have an eye-catching feature that lures people from afar: the bigness of sequoia; the knees of bald cypress; the bizarreness of Joshua tree.

Such signs absorb all of one's wonder.

On the other hand, *every* tree has little intimate signs that point the way to discoveries of the spirit, of art, of mechanics, of astonishment at natural miracles, and of reassurance about life itself in a violent world.

5

When you consider the radical lines drawn by leaf edges, the various ways that bud scales are fitted together, the taste and touch of twigs, the processes of bark, you realize how each fragment of a tree has its own perfection. Somehow all these wondrous parts are put together to create the curious living mechanism we call a tree.

It appears from a tiny capsule more or less the size of a drop of water. It grows with mathematical rhythm, putting out myriads of contact points with the gasses of the atmosphere and minerals of the earth. It erects antennae to catch the power of sunshine. It makes its own food from the elements, and reproduces itself with a shower of seeds. This is an expression of the elemental quality of life that gives wings to the thoughts far beyond the commonplace.

The spirit of a tree is our spirit. Its art is our art. Its color, designs, and the values of its wood and fruit are ours. If you would discover what kind of life is hidden in the shadows of leaves, and behind tough, silent bark, you must find it within yourself. Name tags and identifying features can only point the way.

THE SEVEN REGIONS OF TREE DISCOVERY

The trees of each of these regions are wonderfully different. This is one of the glories of our country.

PICTURE SECTION

Three stars before the name of a tree indicate that it is one of the fourteen keynote trees of the Great American Woods. Two stars and one star are used for the most outstanding trees in the areas where they grow.

THE OAKS_____

In landscaping the world, nature has used more kinds of oak than any other tree. All have acorns, and since no other tree produces this peculiar style of fruit, the acorn is the sure sign of an oak. All acorns have the cup and nut design, yet each is so different that it tells you at a glance what kind of oak it came from. This is seen in the depth of the cup—whether it is a shallow saucer, covers half of the nut, or all but encases the nut that peeks out at the top. The texture of the cup may be rough, spiney, or with smooth scales neatly overlapping. The nut may taper, be rounded, or be long and cylindrical. Color ranges from bright tan to rich mahogany, often seemingly varnished or waxed. The acorn is a masterpiece of finish, as well as a tough and efficient unit for reproduction.

The leaf of the white oak is so well known that people do not realize there are other entirely different shapes of oak leaves. Indeed, it takes mental effort for northerners visiting the South to look upon live oak and laurel oak with their smooth, evergreen, oval leaves as being true oaks at all. The familiar oak leaf deserves its fame. It is like looking from an airplane at an exciting coast with bays and fjords between long peninsulas. Shore lines are fluid; so are the margins of oak leaves. No two are precisely alike, for their deep bays and peninsulas have infinite variety.

The sovereign of the Great American Woods has perfected a body to live in cold or hot, wet or dry, stony place or loam—you see an oak almost everywhere you go. Oak is a positive tree, solidly engineered. Its beauty lies in health and strength, in the simplicity and quality of details.

Distinction goes right to the heart of oak. Its wood is recognizable even to people who pay little heed to the marvelous beauty of wood graining. This is due to vivid markings that swish through the wood, with an eccentric streaming scarcely described by the words "the grain of quartered oak." Their pattern is like that of the aurora borealis when broad glowing festoons of vertical lines dip and sway across the sky. These marks are rays, a feature of wood grain missing from pine. Oak rays are silvery ribbons, set vertically in the wood. They run like the spokes of a wheel from the center of the trunk to the bark. In a cross-cut stump, they form radiating straight lines. Silvery oak rays vary in width at every point, from a half-inch to five inches.

Oaks divide into two groups, the white oaks and the black oaks. It is an interesting sidelight on the mystery of trees that those of our white oak group will not live in Europe when planted there; those of our black oak group live in Europe with vigor. Your first step to enjoy oaks is to see which group your oak belongs to. The following oaks are found in the Great American Woods. See other oaks of the South, Middle West, and West.

WHITE OAK GROUP

Tips of leaf lobes are rounded and smooth, they do not come to a sharp point; and they lack a tiny bristle that black oaks have. Buds are blunt and, like all oaks, are crowded together at the end of their twig. You find few acorns, because they ripen and fall off in one season, and small animals make off with them quickly. Acorns of the White Oak Group are fairly good to eat when roasted. They were an important food of Indians, but we are more fastidious, and let hogs grow fat on them.

You are most likely to see the following white oaks:
***White Oak** takes the least effort to see as it grows from Maine to Texas, and the least effort to call by name, as the bark is the lightest gray of any of the oaks. The white oak acorn is smooth and rounded at the tip like your little finger. You'll discover that same finger form also in the lobes of the white oak leaf. The light gray of the bark is reproduced on the cup of this handsome acorn. Such correspondence of the tints and shapes of different parts of a tree has no botanical importance but it does suggest what we might call a decorator's touch.

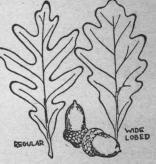

People seldom see a perfect white oak acorn (if you find one, you're entitled to be excited). They grow and fall off in a few

REGULAR   WIDE LOBED

The wide lobe is frequent around New York City.

months and break up rapidly, to vanish into the soil,
returning the loan of nourishment which the tree
borrowed from the ground and packed into them.
This disappearance is assisted by blue jays, crows, squirrels, mice, who find the white oak acorn meat sweet,
and eat or hide the acorns as soon as they fall. Another
reason for acorn scarcity is that it takes some 50 years
for this tree to mature and bear acorns.

Everyone who thinks when he looks can see that trees
come in two styles. Trees with needles (usually evergreen) and trees with broad leaves (usually dropping
in winter). If the broad-leafed race elected an elder
statesman, the white oak should win. It has all the best
qualities that we associate with trees. It forms clean
woods without black shadows but luminous with filtered
sunlight. In these woods the white oak bole reaches high
to get its leaves up to unobstructed sunshine.

In the open field the white oak takes an entirely different form. The trunk is short and heavy, solidly engineered to support mighty, horizontal limbs. Thus the
tree is built broadly and looks as a monarch tree should
look. And the white oak is not only majestic on a big
scale, it contains a hidden star. Cut a twig cleanly across
and peer at the light center of the wood which is the

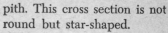

pith. This cross section is not
round but star-shaped.

Put the white oak on your
calendar for mid-spring when
the sun is bright, and see in a
brief space of two or three
days a color effect that is un-
paralleled among trees. The

tiny, opening leaves are a blend of bright pink and silver hairs. The twigs sprout tassels, three to six inches long, that are creamy green. These tassels, tinting the tree with gauzy chartreuse, are the male flowers.

Pioneers looked for the white oak as indicating the best place to build their homes, for its roots go deep and it enjoys rich soil. They followed its advice also in planting corn, knowing that the last frost is over when the pink and silver leaves are the size of the ear of a mouse.

As it's both strong and beautiful, there are more uses for white oak wood than any other timber in the world. It's built into ships, trestles and ties; the oldest whiskey is matured in charred white oak barrels; plank oak floors, paneling, and furniture reveal beautiful graining when they are polished.   *Quercus alba*

The next three trees give you a chance to make some real tree discoveries, and there's definite pride in knowing these when most people don't. All three belong to the White Oak Group, and that is why they are often confused with the white oak described above.

First, get the "feel" of the kind of a spot they grow in. For example, post oak likes the edge of woods, where it's sandy, gravelly, sunny, hot. Chestnut oak (not to be confused with chestnut) likes cool, shadowy ravines, steep rocky places. Swamp white oak likes low wet places.

Post Oak presents an eye-catching leaf with three big squarish lobes like a Maltese cross at the top. The wonder of such a leaf is the way it suggests the shapes of interesting things. Hold it one way—you have a violoncello. The other way it's a dancing doll with big sleeves. This tree's strong wood used to be used for fence posts, but oak lumber is too valuable today. Most of the 600 million fence posts in our country are now red cedar, cypress, black locust. Red hairs grow on under surface of leaf in minute star-shapes, but this takes a lens to see. Post oak gets more common toward the Southwest—abundant in eastern Texas.

Quercus stellata (means star after hairs on leaf)

Chestnut Oak is the big, tough-looking tree with bark in heavy ridges. At the bottom of the furrows between ridges, bark is cinnamon-red. Chestnut oak has largest acorns known on oaks —1½ inches or even 2 inches. This is the acorn to roast and eat. It's the sweetest of all the northern oaks. Look for orange-brown twigs that are not round but angled in an interesting way. Name comes from resemblance to chestnut leaves—large ovals with wavy edges; one of the most beautiful of oak leaves.

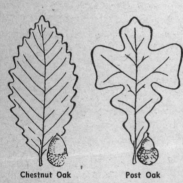

Chestnut Oak   Post Oak

Quercus montana (means mountain, grows high)

Swamp White Oak is the shaggy tree with long-reaching, ungainly limbs. Its bark is loose and sheds in little pieces. Stand off and see the form of this tree. Below the main limbs of the crown there are crooked, down-turned branches covered with leaves throughout their length. These with their bark help to give the shaggy look. Leaf is kite-shaped, wavy around the top like chestnut oak, wedge-shaped near the base like the white oak.

Quercus bicolor

BLACK OAK GROUP

Leaves have sharp angles, lobes are sharp-tipped, bear a tiny bristle. Buds, too, are sharp. You find plenty of acorns because they take two years to ripen, so some always hang on tree. If you see two sizes on same tree, little ones are first year's, big ones are second year's about to fall off. Acorns are bitter, lie around on ground, and slowly disintegrate.

Telling black oaks apart starts you on the path of really seeing trees. All have dark nondescript bark; all have bristle-tipped, sharp-angled leaves; all are good-sized trees. Black oak's inner bark is yellow color; other points of difference between these four are comparative and not so positive. But try it out and catch the feel; you'll have a sense of fresh discovery!

Wood is not so strong, redder in color than white oaks, and markings of grain are not so vivid.

You are most likely to see the following black oaks:

Swamp White Oak

*Red Oak is the oak you encounter most often in the Great American Woods. It is the leader of the four horsemen of the Black Oak Group; other three are black, scarlet, and pin.

Note vertical light strips in the bark of red oak, especially on the upper part of the trunk. These are smooth as though someone had ironed them carelessly lengthwise. The whitish appearance is an optical illusion due to reflection of sky light from the semi-glossy surface. Leaves are dull, dark green, and midrib (that's the big vein in the middle) is often red; underside is smooth—not scurfy or hairy like black oak. Quarter-inch buds are reddish-brown, smooth. Twig is likely to be ridged. Red oak acorns lie around on ground. Handsome, one-inch, oblong nut with white meat (bitter to taste) and shallow saucer at base.

Red oak grows fast (a foot or more in height, an inch wide tree ring per year). Wood is so porous you can blow soap bubbles with a stick of it. Boston's parkway system shows what a clean street tree it makes. Around New York this is the commonest oak of the woods.

Quercus borealis

Black Oak is a specific member of the black oak group. This is confusing. Think of it here as *the* black oak. It should be called yellow oak because penknife through black outer bark shows yellow inner bark for quick identification. Lining of acorn cup is bright yellow. Acorn meat is yellow, and so bitter that animals spurn it. Leaves are wider toward top, and broadly pear-shaped compared to its brother red oak whose leaves are wider in middle and outline is oval. Buds are grayish, hairy, and angled. These ridged buds are an interesting point that takes close observation, but easy to see if you look for it.

Beautiful colorful effect is crimson of black oak's unfolding leaves in spring—rich red, soft, hairy, with droplets of sparkling sap. The bright yellow encountered in this tree is valuable tannin—a chemical used for tanning leather.

Quercus velutina (means velvety, refers to gray hairiness of buds)

Pin Oak is the trim, straight shade tree used in suburbs, parks, towns more often than any other oak. One sign of pin oak is the mass of down-turned branches—sometimes touching the ground. However, these may be pruned off by alert park department. It has a staccato accent with sharp, pin-like twig pattern, and deeply cut, angular leaves. Smaller than other oaks—buds are tiny, ⅛ inch, angled and sharp, leaves and acorns little and finely sculptured. Name comes from its tough pin-like twigs used as wooden pegs instead of nails in square timbers of old barns. *Quercus palustris*

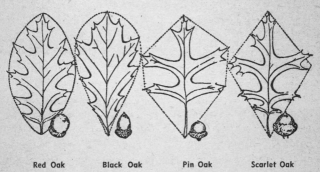

Red Oak   Black Oak   Pin Oak   Scarlet Oak

Scarlet Oak can vie with any other tree when it unveils richest red of the fall. Holds its leaves longer than maples, and color is deeper, richer, but not so flaming. Between New York and Atlantic City in October people are dazzled by scarlet oaks. Also seen through Middle West, but not in Appalachian Mountains. Otherwise tree is easily confused with pin oak, having similar deeply cut, angular leaves. Lacks pin-like twigs of pin oak. Leaves, buds are larger. Inner bark is pinkish.   *Quercus coccinea*

Scrub Oak is ignored by lumbermen but not by people who enjoy the crooked, picturesque oaks of gravelly, rocky places and hilltops. Leaves come in so many shapes a single tree gives you enough eccentric symmetry to fill your sketch book. In fall these leaves produce a motley of reds and yellows. There's nothing like the leaf whimsies and crooked-twig enchantment of this tree.

Quercus ilicifolia

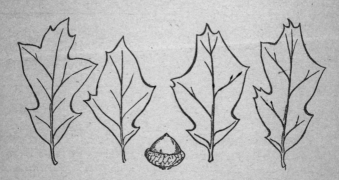

Scrub oak bears many whimsical patterns.

THE MAPLES_____

If you would see perfection, go look at the maple. It is like truth made into the form of a tree. From over-all proportion to the smallest detail every part fits together in perfect balance. This gives that quality of an organism known as health. Out of air and water the living cell has created seed wings for the maple like those of a soaring bird. It has endowed the wood with whirlings and ripplings like light upon the surface of water. Above all, maples have fitness and strength. This is the quality of our land. Sugar maple is distinctly American; it will not grow in England. It must have pure, fresh air; it is not a city tree. Sugar maple is the insignia of a Vermont hillside, where it blends into the New England scene along with a man-made barn softened by rain and moss. Red maple is the breath of a bog and the frame of a pond, a consonance not so perfect anywhere else in the world.

Know the maples, one from another. In a lifetime you will perhaps see only half a dozen. All bear the family expression in the pattern of their leaves. All have inherited the two-winged seed idea which, like opening scissor blades, takes different angles in the different kinds of maples.

It is symmetrical because every detail grows in dupli-
cate. When it puts forth a bud, this is matched by a twin
bud on exactly the opposite side of the twig. This leads
to branch opposite branch, leaf opposite leaf. This plan
of growth is found also in seed and leaf patterns, where
angles and curves of one side seem to be reflected like
mirror images on the opposite side.

You will find the three leading American maples—
sugar, red, and silver, everywhere from Maine to Texas,
and often more numerous than any other hardwood. In
suburban parks and along streets maples are the most
planted of any kind of tree. These are your trees, enjoy
them.

(See also box elder under Middle West).

★★★Sugar Maple is most successful tree, and con-
tender for the title of the most beautiful tree in the
world. Its wood is bright and polishes attractively to
make furniture with an aura all its own. This tree forms
a practically perfect oval. Its fruit has the grace and

streamlining of the wing of an airplane.
Its fall colors rival the highest color
keys of the sunset. Its leaf is a geometric
masterpiece.

The Great American Woods is decorated throughout with maple leaves. Two
kinds of maple march side by side, sugar
and red. Both are so abundant that you
can always find the two kinds of leaves
within a few steps to hold and compare.
The sugar has five lobes that point

Collecting
maple syrup

out, widespreading. Angles between lobes are rounded.

Now compare that leaf with the red maple. This usually has three lobes that point forward, making the leaf
narrower. The edges are not so smooth but have more
teeth. The angle between the lobes is sharp. In brief, if
the angle forms a U, it's a sugar; if it forms a V, it's a red.

In the early spring when the snow may still be on the
ground, and the sun is warm on the bark by day while
the nights are below freezing, the sugar maple can be
tapped for sugar sap. Boiling it down we get the grand
American maple syrup and maple sugar. The pipe that
taps the sap is driven into the trunk four feet above
the ground, and, by expansion under sunlight and con-
traction during cold nights, the wood acts as a pump!

Sugar maple is queen of firewoods, doesn't throw out
sparks. Keeps burning cheerily and makes fine, clean,
white ashes, delightful smell, and flame has pretty play
of colors.   *Acer saccharum*

★**Red Maple** is the tree to know if you were condemned
to know but a single tree. Most red maples are medium

Sugar Maple   Red Maple

sized, intimate—you can reach the branches. Hold the
tip of a growing twig (do not tear it off) and see the
buds. They are rich, smooth, crimson. The flower buds
are bunched around twigs, fat, prominent—their red, gold,
orange sparkling with sap when starting to open is a
sight you would want to go half way around the world
to see. This happens early, same time as pussy willows.
Leaves are light green on top, whitish below, making
sharp V in the angle between the lobes. The pale undersides give the flash of white over a tree when a sudden
breeze turns up the leaves. At all times of year this tree
shows red somewhere. Leaf stem is bright red. Fall colors
are red and yellow. Flowers in spring are gauzy red, and
this when seen against a deep blue sky is a color combination you'll marvel at.

Straight, quick-growing, easy-to-transplant red maple
makes a fine street tree where there is moisture. Bark is
clean, light gray in upper part of trunk and main limbs—
often so smooth and light it can be mistaken for beech.
The unique wood grains known as birds-eye maple or
curly maple are sometimes hidden in this tree. These are
not evident from outward appearances, but who would
cut down his red maple to find out?   *Acer rubrum*

Silver Maple is well named after the bright silver underside of its leaves. These are fancy, decorative. Lobes are
long, sharply toothed, cut in almost to center of leaf.
This tree has big, conspicuous clusters of plump flower
buds that make twigs in winter look as though something were the matter with them. Silver maples bloom
earliest of any tree. Seed wings are big, wide-spread like

Silver Maple

those of a floating seagull. Trunk divides into long, curving limbs, slightly resembling elm. Many silver maples were sold to last generation by nurserymen who recommended speed of growth; therefore, you see them around older houses. But silver maple is brittle and wind tears them apart through the years. Silver and red maples are known as soft maples.

Acer saccharinum

Black Maple

Black Maple is a version of sugar maple with small, dark leaves suggesting sketches of sugar maple leaves simplified, with clean, straight edges, no fancy teeth. These leaves tend to droop and curl. Often seen around towns in South Dakota and Iowa, and many around Philadelphia.

Acer nigrum

★**Moosewood** is a revelation of interesting bark. On twigs and branches this is semi-glossy, exactly the color and texture of a green olive, marked with white lines, as though someone had stroked it with a piece of chalk. This bark is alive, and that fact keeps it satin smooth. Outside bark on most trees is dead, breaks into corky surface when rent by expanding wood, or outer layer of dead skin peels off, as on birches. Moosewood's juicy sugary bark and buds are eaten by deer and moose. Leaves are large, rounded like a deep bowl. This tree is of the wild woods, along mountain streams, in cool, shadowy, high places where you may think there's only a tangle of underbrush. It's worth climbing a wooded hill to see.   *Acer pensylvanicum*

Both pheasant and Mountain Maple are found in shady woods.

Mountain Maple is easily taken for a young red maple, but leaves are rougher, darker, rounder. Bark is red-brown, twigs are hairy. Often the dominant tree of the mountain underbrush where ruffed grouse finds cover. Found side by side with moosewood, these two little maples have probably made more mountain hikers in eastern states sopping wet after a rain than any other woodland plant.

Acer spicatum

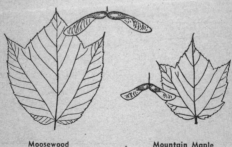

Moosewood   Mountain Maple

You will often see the following maples on lawns and residential streets:

Norway Maple's leaf is nearly the same shape and size as sugar maple's, and has the same rounded angle between lobes, but underside is dark, glossy green, not dull whitish. Another difference is milky sap in leaf stem. Casts deep shade—it's hard to grow grass under this tree.

Acer platanoides

Schwedler Maple—a version of Norway maple with leaves bronze-red in spring. Popular tree around Minneapolis. Fine row in Brooklyn Botanic Garden.

Acer schwedleri

Sycamore Maple is the sycamore of Europe. Marvelous styling of maple leaf. Just stare at its full-rounded, heavily toothed lobes.

Acer pseudo-platanus

Japanese Cutleaf Maple is the tiny, wine-red little maple with fancy, deeply cut leaves extended like fingers of a child's hand.

Acer japonicum

Sycamore Maple

Japanese Maple

THE ELMS

★★★**American Elm** is America's most vivid tree. Here is a superb diagram of the way trees can be fluid fountains. Air and water united by light rush upward out of the dark earth, throwing out branches like a skyrocket sparkling with green leaves against the sky. The most characteristic form of the American elm is that of a column of water mounting with tremendous force. At about one-third of its height the column splits into several branches that arch outward gradually as they mount, until at the crest they dome upward as the thrust is lost to gravity and then pour earthward at the point where the spray vanishes. When man erects a fine fountain at great expense, people come to wonder at it. Nature has distributed these elegant tree fountains all over the eastern half of the United States, and people have not been blind to this either, because elm, purely for its beauty, has been planted along the streets and around the squares of towns more than any other tree. It is the keynote of many New England villages— the tall, steep curves of the branches meeting high above the street as over the nave of a cathedral.

Face under Elm bud (enlarged) is a sleepy one.

Strangely, there are no natural groves purely of elms. They mingle with bushes and other trees in woods and hedgerows. In eastern states elm is the commonest tree seen. It survives better than most trees where man disturbs the countryside. This is partly because its wood is not one of the big demand timbers of the sawmill, and partly because people love the elm as it flourishes in open field, meadow or street as well as in the woods.

American Elm

If calling a tree by name were all there is to knowing it, no more need be said about the elm. But due to its popularity as a tree-fountain, most people overlook details that are unique and fun to see.

Elm leaf is an example of off-center symmetry. It is lopsided at the base, from which the blade curves, forming the segment of a spiral shell. This is the same curve as that of the graceful limbs on which they are borne. Elm leaf has double teeth; it is rough to the touch, and dark blue-green compared to the brighter leaf-green of other trees.

The eccentric swing of the leaf is repeated in the bud. This is tipped to one side, above an oval mark in the twig bark that has the features of a face winking at you. Bud and face look like a rakish fellow wearing a hat.

The twig on which this whimsy is set, although slender and often pendant like a string, is zig-zag. This is because the elm produces no bud squarely at the end of the twig to give it a forward thrust. Therefore, the twig must elongate at an angle—first on one side, then on other side, from successive buds.   *Ulmus americana*

The American elm is so much a part of our country's landscape wherever trees are enjoyed east of the Rockies that there is consternation at the possibility of losing them. The Dutch elm disease fungus attacks through a broken or decayed place. Leaves wilt, drop off. Tree should be cut down and burned. This malady, confined for many years to area around New York, is spreading today. More swiftly destructive is bark disease caused by a virus now killing many fine old elms in Middle West and South. Hope that this can be controlled before this tree disappears from our lives like the chestnut is based on recent discovery that virus is spread by leaf-hopping insect.

No other kind of elm has the form and elegance of the American, so, although others may resist the disease, they are not substitutes. Each of the following four elms has individual characteristics that are unusual and interesting to know about.

Slippery Elm can be spotted in winter by twigs and buds with iridescent red hairs. In spring bark slips when you touch it. Inner bark is gummy, good to taste, nutri-

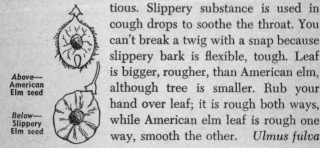

Above—
American
Elm seed

Below—
Slippery
Elm seed

tious. Slippery substance is used in cough drops to soothe the throat. You can't break a twig with a snap because slippery bark is flexible, tough. Leaf is bigger, rougher, than American elm, although tree is smaller. Rub your hand over leaf; it is rough both ways, while American elm leaf is rough one way, smooth the other.   *Ulmus fulva*

Rock Elm (also called cork elm) has form like a hickory with trunk continuous from base to top, contrasted to American elm that divides trunk into several big limbs. Branches are shaggy with thick, irregular corky ridges like those on sweet gum. This tree gets its name from hardness of wood (better wood than other elms). It has interlocking fibers, hard to split, makes mallets and wheel hubs. Seen most in Michigan, Minnesota, and around Great Lakes.   *Ulmus thomasi*

English Elm has heavy trunk and limbs that go out at right angles, like an oak in weight and character. This is Europe's common elm. You see it in older parks such as Gramercy Park, New York, and there are some fine ones on Boston Common.   *Ulmus campestris*

Siberian Elm (close relative of Chinese elm) is one of the fastest growing trees in the United States. Trunk swells an inch a year, height increases some three feet a year. Small leaves cast gay, mottled shade. Tree's chief defect is brittleness of branches. Provides shade in hot, dry places where other trees are scrawny, and is most widely used street and shade tree in cities and towns along U.S. Highway 81, from Texas to South Dakota. Also main windbreak trees planted by U. S. Forest Service on Great Plains.   *Ulmus pumila*

THE NUT TREES_____

The good wood of our nut trees has been felt by more American hands than any other wood. Rich, chocolate-brown gunstocks are black walnut. Axe handles are hickory. Such wood stands sudden shock with a peculiar twang of elasticity. It never warps or bends from alignment. It is smooth, splinterless, good to feel.

The nut tells its tree as clearly as the acorn tells an oak and the two-winged seed a maple. Both walnut and hickory have the hard-shelled seed encased in a tough husk. The kernel packs food value measured in protein and calories surpassing anything else that grows on wild trees of our woods. Ounce for ounce black walnut has eight times the protein of milk; hickory nuts four times. This delicious food keeps raining down, and the man who keeps his trees reaps their harvests, whereas the man who makes a gunstock or axe handle of his no longer has such crops. But it takes energy and patience to crack nuts and pick out the kernels, and in a packaged food era we miss the healthy fun of nutting that used to be as great a feature of the fall season as gathering pumpkins.

Bitternut (left)
and Mockernut
faces (enlarged)

A small surprise awaits you here. Nut trees have funny faces. These are best seen in winter. Take in hand a twig and look closely below any bud. Impressed in the bark you'll see the tiny face of a horse or camel. On walnuts these faces are clear, neat, with pads of hair like well-clipped forelocks. On hickories the faces are larger, with elongated noses, often lopsided and eccentric. The funny faces tell you what tree it is by their expressions, the way you know people.

***Shagbark Hickory** (also called shellbark) is the tree you have to go out into the country to find. It does not like impure air, and it cannot be hurried, so you seldom find it in the city. In the field  or on the hillside it grows slowly, solidly, where it can put roots deep into nutritious soil conditioned naturally by time. It is the companion of white oak, and like that tree it was a sign of a good place for pioneer settlers to build their homes and plant crops.

No other tree has bark like this well-named tree. You'll know a mature shagbark instantly when you see a strong, tall trunk whose bark is loosened so that long, hard, gray

Shagbark Hickory

strips warp out like shingles that have become unnailed on an old house. These strips are all lengths, even up to four feet, and may be loose both top and bottom. Despite its hardness, this peculiar bark is not brittle but elastic. A strip that appears to be on the point of dropping off the tree may hang on for years. If a house were to become loose like this, it would promptly be a shambles, but nature has put no nails or bolts into the shagbark to rust, and this marvelously weatherproof bark builds a picturesque tree that will long outlive the men around it. This feature of a tree whose nuts are so sweet protects its chance for survival. A squirrel, who would not hesitate to strip it clean of nuts, encounters this series of abattis that makes it difficult to run up the trunk.

Elasticity is also a feature of the tough wood; therefore, hickory does not make such good paneling and furniture as maple or pine, which have to be formed, but is used chiefly as axe handles, plows, barrel staves, athletic equipment including baseball bats. You can hear this beautiful wood ring true when you bounce a hickory bat on a rock. Best of all fire logs, shagbark is the king wood for heat. It is long burning, sparkless, with clean ash and beautiful flame.

This tree does not shag its bark until it bears nuts, after forty years. You can tell a young shagbark from the older ones by its leaf with only five leaflets, and its hard gray bark. In winter it has an oval bud of buff suede, and the tree detective will peer closely to see that the scales around this bud have sharp projections at their tips—a sure sign of shagbark.   *Carya ovata*

The **Big Shellbark** or **Kingnut** is a version of shagbark found west of the Alleghenies; it is a larger tree with a bigger nut. This tree is so distinctive that by the time it reaches the Middle West it may have leaves almost two feet long and bear huge nuts.   *Carya laciniosa*

Pignut is a fine hickory with an unfortunate name. Common in northern states, it escapes attention because bark is not exciting like shagbark. Smooth to touch— smooth leaves and twigs, small round bud on twig tip; even bark is smoothish. Splendid hickory wood; one of three used for scythe and axe handles, baseball bats, and wherever good hickory is used. In order of excellence the best tool handle hickories are shagbark, pignut, and mockernut. Nut is pearshaped, like a little fig; smooth, thin shell, edible but sometimes bitter.

Carya glabra   **Pignut Hickory**

Mockernut grows in northern states as fine tree with shagbark and pignut. Its wood also makes tool handles. But mockernut has several remarkable points of difference. Big, round bud on twig tip is silky gray suede, has remarkably artistic texture and soft tint. Leaves and twigs are aromatic, delightfully fragrant. Nut is big and inviting. This gives tree its name as shell is mighty and contains slight amount of meat to disentangle; utterly disappointing. Someone with sense of humor named tree. This hickory, stepping down from New England hills, adopts small, scrubby form, becomes part of tangle back of south Atlantic sand dunes with holly and live oak. A strange place to find hickory.   *Carya alba*

Bitternut has sulphur yellow bud on twig tips; slender, curved like a scythe blade, sparkling with amber dots.

This bud is naked; that is, without covering scales; you can see the tiny folds of the leaf. Bitternut is a stately shade tree, transplants well, grows faster than other hickories. Nuts are so bitter even squirrels spurn them. Wood is poor hickory but good for smoking hams. Often in moist ground in New England, and this is the commonest hickory in Iowa, Kansas, Nebraska.   *Carya cordiformis*

Bitternut Hickory

Pecan produces the only million dollar crop from our wild trees. It comes so excellent in nature that man is stimulated to select best trees for breeding, which today goes ahead creating bigger nuts, thinner shells, more delicate flavor. In woods of Georgia, Alabama, Texas, pecan trees soar above 100 feet. Many of them are seen planted in the Middle West and southward, around older plantations. Branches are very long; when not pruned lower ones slope down, giving peculiar reaching-down aspect to tree. Value is in the nut crop; wood is poor but smokes good hams, as does mockernut. *Carya pecan*

BLACK WALNUT

★★★**Black Walnut** is as American as the Indian. But among our big, valuable hardwoods it is the one which surprisingly few people can call by name, because neither bark nor leaf nor outline spell black walnut in bold letters. So this is a good place to discover some not so obvious details that arouse wonder and interest in the reading of a tree.

The surest token is the nut. This can be seen on the tree at the end of summer when black walnut leaves drop off ahead of all other leaves. Then for a couple of weeks black walnut has a peculiar sort of conspicuousness. It stands out stark and leafless when other trees are fully in leaf or turning brilliant colors. The tall dome of branches is studded with the big, round nuts black against the sky.

Leaves are multiple and stand apart on long limbs that reach far out from the main trunk. Sunlight filters through, so that shadows of black walnut have the texture of mottled sunlight, compared to dense shadows cast by maples. The light green of walnut foliage contrasts sharply with the black bark of the long limbs, gives black walnut an accent all its own.

Black Walnut leaf

A sure sign of black walnut is the pith. Slice a twig and see the light brown cross-parti-

tions like ties of a railroad track. Butternut has a similar
peculiar pith, but partitions are heavier, closer, and dark
brown.

Nuts are unique and frustrating. Husk stains hands
brown but is delightfully fragrant. Nut shell has metallic
hardness; when shattered with hammer the kernel is
found hidden in a labyrinth. But flavor is like no other
food in the world, and because it's not lost with cooking,
makes good ice cream, candy, cake. Picking out kernels
is a home industry in eastern Tennessee where this wild
tree-crop is at its best. There's little black walnut to be
seen in New England, plenty in the Middle West.

Juglans nigra

*Butternut (also called white walnut) has the face
of a solemn camel with a downy brow below each bud.
An amusing and sure way to know the tree. Butternut
grows singly in rich hillside pastures and along roads in
New England, central New York State. It's a small version of black walnut, with light, feathery leaves and
black branches. An intimate tree compared to the giant
black walnut. You can reach its lower branches to see
the faces and hairy twigs, and smell leaf fragrance. Nut
is small oval with husk covered with red, sticky
hairs. Ironbound meat comes out in crumbs, but
these are deliciously oily. Too bad butternut
kernels are so meager, hard to extract; they have
the highest food value of any of our nuts. Name
white walnut refers to the clean, white wood.

Juglans cinerea

Chambered pith of
Butternut twig

English Walnut provides the round, rumpled nuts in your nut bowl. Shells are so thin you can break them with your hands. It should be possible to breed our black walnut with such a shell. The original English walnuts had hard, thick shells, tiny kernels; for centuries men selected best trees in Persia, Spain, Japan—see the resulting walnuts we have today. English walnut picked up its name merely by coming to us via England—it should be called Persian walnut. A fine walnut tree with a nut crop worth millions of dollars. You often see it planted; people are proud of their English walnuts. Big orchards in southern California. See page 222. *Juglans regia*

Chestnut has a long oval leaf with waving scallops tipped with bristles that point forward. It is a masterpiece of rhythm and proportion. The middle vein runs precisely through the center of the leaf, and side veins run parallel from mid-rib to bristles. You'll see lots of chestnut leaves on a walk through hilly Appalachian woods but they do not grow on a tree. They are shoots springing out of a big trunk where one of America's noblest trees used to grow. A bark disease destroyed the chestnuts with their superb wood and burs of good nuts. But they still struggle to live, and perhaps the next generation will see the sucker switches from old roots overcoming the deadly malady and turning into trees again. Meanwhile, enjoy the leaves as a bit of unsurpassed woodland art.

Castanea dentata   Chestnut leaf

★★★**American Beech** can always be recognized by its broad bole and strong limbs apparently made of aluminum. The bark is thin and alive so that it stretches as the tree grows, forming silvery smoothness on trunk and branches from top to bottom.

Beech is the brightest of the big trees, for not only does the bark have a silvery glow, but also the leaves are light, glossy green and, held in flat mosaic layers tipped toward the sun, reflect brightness of the sky. In winter these leaves cling on—crisp, shimmering, golden. On a clear winter's day when a bright sun is shining across the snow, beech offers an unforgettable spectacle. If you are an artist at heart, make a note right now not to miss this phenomenal effect of tints: silvery bark against crystal white snow, golden leaves against a blue sky.

Beech buds are unique. No other bud is so long (almost an inch) and so sharp (you can prick your finger). They're like tightly rolled spindles, made of rich tan leather, tooled with a crisscross design. Touch the twig to see these buds, and you discover a bit of the finest tree jewelry.

American Beech

Compare beech with white oak. They are members of the same family, yet bark, buds, and leaves are so different they are never confused. However, both trees tend to hold their leaves all winter, especially younger ones. Both trees are powerfully built—wide trunks in the open, tall pillars in the woods.

It's only a step in evolution from an acorn to a beechnut. Just imagine that beechnut's prickly husk is the cup of an acorn that in this case, encloses the whole unit. Inside this, two nuts are curiously shaped as sharp-angled triangles. These are sweet and edible, deliciously oily as though buttered, but people seldom get a chance to sample this titbit because squirrels, deer, bluejays get to them first.

Beechnut contains two delicious kernels.

The oil throughout a beech is reputed to resist electricity, and therefore a beech is struck by lightning far less often than other trees. *Fagus grandifolia*

Copper Beech, a variation of a European beech, is often seen in city parks. Leaves are glossy, copper-red, and, in reflecting light, give off red flashes in the sun. One of our most beautiful trees.

Fagus sylvatica var. atropunicea

Slender,
pointed buds of
American Beech

THE ASHES_____

Ash plays an active part in our everyday lives through tennis rackets, baseball bats, snowshoes, bushel baskets, butter tubs, and oars. Such clean, easily formed wood comes from healthy trees, a pride of our countryside. Because ash is mild and unsensational, it attracts less attention. The multiple leaves are like walnut or hickory. When these come in pairs, with leaf opposite leaf on the branch, it is a sure sign of ash. White ash is the most abundant; chances are that is the one you see, except in prairie states and westward where green ash abounds in the moist ground near streams or springs. Green ash is the State Tree of almost treeless North Dakota. The various kinds of ash have names as though tagged with colored ribbons.

★★★**White Ash** is the most anonymous of the Big Fourteen of the Great American Woods. It does not call out to you loudly as do trees with acorns, maple leaves, birch bark. But though ash speaks quietly, it speaks so clearly that this is the first tree you should discover and recognize beyond the obvious ones.

The parts of ash are so finely wrought that, separated from the tree, each is a thing of beauty in itself. Put together, these artistic details build a tree that wins first prize in tree architecture.

The trunk is utterly simple, lifting the tree upward out of the ground with the harmony of a temple column. This is unmarred by old knots or branches. Around this trunk ridges of bark form a diamond pattern like a woven basket. Ridges are flat on top as though a builder had used a plane to smooth them off a bit. Ash bark is so dark, almost black, in color that you may have to look twice to appreciate its remarkable pattern; it is rough and broken because the outside doesn't stretch but bursts as the trunk expands.

The most stylish of tree buds are more or less inconspicuous because they are not bright and colorful. However, very dark brown or black suede can be elegant, so look carefully. Lay hold of a winter branch, and see how buds grow exactly opposite each other along the twig. This ash twig is heavy and rigid compared to the slender, wiry twigs of the birches or the pendant strings of elm. This sturdy twig has tiny little dark blobs of buds in pairs, opposite each other. Let your fingers run along the smooth, graceful, slightly scalloped twig to the buds at the end. Here are three buds fitted tightly together: two small hemispheres hold in a bowl between them a small dome, capped with an abrupt point. This adornment has a slender crescent like a half-moon underneath, where a leaf stem was attached. The ef-

White Ash

fect is that of a handsome twig finished off at the tip with an architectural design of curves and terraces. Once you are familiar with these big twigs and their end buds, you can always tell an ash by them. Also, make a note to take a look in April just before the buds open and behold their rich suede studded with glistening amber.

Ash leaves are multiple. Leaflets are so large that, seen high up in the tree, they do not appear to be units of multiple leaves, but rather as the standard ovals of other trees such as birch or elm.

Most plants combine stamen and pistil (male and female) in one flower, but ash separates the sexes as do animals so that an individual ash tree produces either male or female flowers. It's like holly and poplar in this respect. Thus only the female trees bear seeds, single winged, compared to maple seeds that have two wings. Winged ash seeds are exquisitely graceful, like tiny canoe paddles. In fact, ash wood is so tough and elastic that it makes the best paddles, as well as tennis rackets, hoe and

rake handles, bows and arrows. Ash wood burns while still green because sap is inflammable.

Ash is a member of an aristocratic southern family, the Olives. It marched north with three colorful shrub members of the same family: privet, forsythia, and lilac.   *Fraxinus americana*

White Ash seeds
resemble tiny
canoe paddles.

Red Ash has curious details that give it its name. Buds are covered with dense red-brown velvet; also twigs and undersurfaces of leaves have red hairs. Inner bark of young branches is red. Grows separately in wetter places at the foot of the hills whereas white ash is up on hillsides and in the upland woods with maple, beech, basswood. *Fraxinus pennsylvanica*

Green Ash is the western version of red ash. It differs in not having velvety hairs on buds, twigs, leaves. Underside of white ash leaf is white; the underside of green ash is green. This is the ash everyone out West knows. It grows in shelter belts on prairies, and in the Far West in stream bottoms and on river banks of dry country. *Fraxinus lanceolata*

Blue Ash has 4-angled twigs. Look for this curiosity made by corky angles of bark. Sap turns blue in water. Tree is common in dry limestone places of Tennessee and Kentucky and around lower Ohio valley. *Fraxinus quadrangulata*

Black Ash is one of the slenderest of woods trees, stretching high with small trunk diameter. Buds are jet black. It is most northern of ashes, abundant in swampy ground in northern New England and New York. Wood is tougher, more elastic than other ashes. After soaking wood, if you bend and pound it, the annual rings separate; make flexible slats for weaving pack basket. *Fraxinus nigra*

SYCAMORE

***Sycamore** (also called plane tree or buttonwood)
is the old giant. You know it at a glance by the white,
purple, and gray patchwork quilt of its bark. Upper trunk
and lower part of limbs may be smooth, bright white all
over. This dramatic bark has unforgettable splendor. On
a clear winter day, when lighted by brightness from
snow, it is like nothing else in treedom. (For colorful,
mottled bark see also eucalyptus and madrone.) Sycamore grows only the inner layer of its bark every year.
This living bark becomes white on exposure to the sun,
and the bark of previous years, not growing and therefore
not expanding to fit around the bigger trunk, is forced off
the tree in patches. In effect, the tree is bursting its
breeches. Varied tints are due to the number of years' exposure of the older layers before they fall off. Sunlight
turns bark chemicals gold, brown, and blue-gray.

Sycamore contends with tulip
tree for the title of biggest tree
of the Great American Woods.
In Indiana, headquarters state
for sycamore, it comes 150 feet
tall, with trunk 10 feet in diameter. Sycamores grow along
stream banks in the Ohio River
and lower Mississippi valleys in
such abundance that seen from
an airplane, the courses of

Sycamore

streams are marked by lines of white trunks.

When looking at the bark effect in winter, you will notice one-inch balls of its fruit dangling on strings among the upper branches. This gives the tree one of its favorite names, buttonball. The true American sycamore, growing along streams of the countryside, has white patches and single balls. Other kinds,

Sycamore leaf-stem fits over bud like candle-snuffer.

planted in cities, have two or more balls in clusters, and the patches are brown. See London Plane Tree page 89.

Sycamore leaves remind you of maple leaves but are larger and lobes are shallower. Most interesting fact about this leaf is the swollen end of its stem. Pull it off the twig and you'll see that this is a hollow cone that covers the winter bud as an old-fashioned snuffer covers a candle flame. This bud does not have overlapping scales like most buds; it's like a smooth, red-brown tam-o'-shanter. All the way round the base of the bud the twig is terraced where the leaf stem was attached.

Despite its greatness, sycamore does not grow symmetrically. To make its appearance even more ragged, this patriarch is torn by a fungus disease. It is the first of our hardwoods to grow on earth, having survived millions of years to attract us with its bark and balls. Zigzag branches are irregular and angular as though striking out from the huge trunk. The wood is hard to split, and it's clean, white, odorless and tasteless—fine for butchers' blocks.   *Platanus occidentalis*

"Button ball" of Sycamore tree

TULIP TREE

★★★**Tulip Tree** is supreme for bigness and harmony among our hardwoods. Tulip tree grows among other forest trees, never forming pure cathedral-like groves that make sequoia so awesome. Thus people of eastern United States don't realize that they won't have to travel to the Pacific Coast to see one of the world's finest forest trees. Its trunk pours straight upward, uninterrupted by limbs, to a great height. Passing motorists can enjoy some of the biggest, spared by the axe, as features of parkways in eastern and middle western cities. In upper Manhattan are some old tulip trees occupying 100 square feet of the world's most expensive real estate.

In winter, tips of bare branches hold up broad champagne goblets, silhouetted high against the sky. Twigs curve deftly to hold these upright. They are the winter remains of the "tulips" which bloomed on the tree in June.

These tulips, which give the tree its name, are actually magnolia flowers. But since the petals are light green on

the outside and grow high among the leaves, not many people have discovered them. If you can find a flower on the ground you will see that a tree famous for its trunk and not its flower has as harmonious and elegant a blossom as a water lily. Note the deep orange splashes on inside of petals.

Tulip tree leaf and duck-bill bud

Tulip tree leaf is broad and clean, and

flutters in the wind as do leaves of trembling aspen. This superficial resemblance has given tree the name of yellow poplar, although it is really a magnolia. The leaf is a masterpiece of design. Because it has a squared-off summit, it suggests the primitive simplicity of Inca architecture as contrasted with the Gothic style of the maple leaf. There are no sharp angles. The truncated leaf is not harshly square like the belfry of a country church, but the top line is drawn as the curve of a saddle.

Tulip tree "cone." Each "petal" bears a seed.

In every part tulip tree is fluent. It holds its immensity on tiptoe, standing lightly on its feet. The wood is light weight; the trunk is so tall it has slender proportions; the leaves dance to the slightest breeze; the roots are tender and fleshy and do not lay hold of rocky land with ironbound power as roots of white oak and hickory do.

Another expression of this smooth, fluid nature is the winter bud. Instead of overlapping scales there are two outer scales, flat and broad like the bill of a duck. These make a valve, in the same way a clam shell makes a valve. When there is pressure inside, the two scales open like a mouth, and out come spring leaves.

The charm of the tree is ingrained. Its wood takes a high polish, and because it is white, easy to work, and comes in wide boards, it makes wonderful paneling or veneer. This is the wood used for hat blocks as it doesn't absorb moisture under steaming process.

Harmonious tulip tree has a scientific name that is a musical one to hear yourself say.

Liriodendron tulipifera

BASSWOOD

★★★**Basswood** (also called linden) is fun to know because of its remarkable bag of tricks. People who think all Chinamen look alike might confuse this tree with elm—tall trunk, shallow-fissured bark of no distinction, long limbs reaching up at steep angles. The bark is lighter gray than elm, and basswood leans while elm grows straight up.

The surest sign of basswood is the unique flower-fruit apparatus. In early summer, weeks after other trees have flowered, basswood breaks out, a harvest of light yellow, star-shaped, half inch flowers. These dangle in clusters of six or so from a stem that comes out of the center of a peculiar, special leaf, resembling a 4-inch length of stiff green ribbon.

These flowers, fairly dripping with nectar, have such honeyed fragrance you can smell a basswood nearby. Bees are so intoxicated with joy over basswood flowers that, with all their buzzing, you may even hear a basswood as well as smell it. If there's a hollow in the tree, it's a prime place for a beehive. The flowers turn into round, hard nuts the size of small peas, that dangle from the center of the ribbon-leaf, which becomes a sail for the fruit in October. The contrivance is nicely balanced, with heavy little seeds swinging below the leaf. You can find these hard, green-gray little "peas" on the ground any time of the year. They decay slowly and may take several years to sprout a baby basswood.

The tree's name has nothing to do with gamey sea fish.

It is derived from bast, fibers that are used to weave mats or ropes or to wind around split handle of a hoe or rake. This bast, or inner bark, encloses the trunk of the tree like a tough, stringy shirt, and is also used for weaving into chair-bottoms and baskets.

Basswood buds are rich red or a deep red and green combination; a colorful tone-blend to capture in drapery or wallpaper. Only two scales show, and you can instantly spot a basswood by the way one of these bulges out, making the bud lopsided. This eccentricity carries over into the leaf, which also bulges out on one side becoming lopsided, but with a fluid curve as though the whole leaf were gracefully turning to one side.

More people have probably touched natural basswood (without knowing it) than any other unfinished wood. It is clean, white, odorless, unsplintery; it glues well and steams and bends easily. It is good for small things your hand often touches, such as toy airplanes, strawberry baskets, yardsticks, wooden partitions of honeycombs, Venetian blinds. Smooth, compact straight-graining makes good artists' charcoal.

Tilia americana

Basswood leaf (above) and special sail-leaf with fruit (below)

Common Linden, seen in city parks, is smaller than basswood; has round, pretty head, round leaves. These are heart-shaped and lopsided at base like American basswood. This is Europe's common linden that gave the name to Berlin's Unter den Linden. *Tilia vulgaris*

BLACK LOCUST

★★★**Black Locust** is our most eccentric tree. It plays dead most of the year because its leaves come out much later and fall off long before those of other trees. The leafless black locust is tall, gaunt with a battlefield look as though a vulture should be leering from a broken limb. In fact the tree is easily identified by its stark silhouette.

When black locust finally puts forth leaves, they seem to sprout, not from buds, but mysteriously from inside the tree. The absence of visible buds, the callous place in the bark of a twig, and a pair of short, wicked prickles are clear identification of this tree.

The multiple leaves are ten inches long. Small egg-shaped leaflets are arranged in pairs. In the rain or at night leaflets fold up like a book, the leaf stem droops,

and thus in gloomy weather the tree looks forlorn. But when young leaves are fully exposed in the sunlight, the foliage of black locust is the most beautiful green of our hardwoods. The latest leaflets to unfurl at the tips are bright yellow-green; those which have been exposed to the light for a week are darker blue-green. This gives the foliage a rich duotone, especially effective in copses of young black locusts often seen along country roads.

The bark of an old black locust is deeply

Black Locust   furrowed, contributing to the rugged aspect. Heavy, disorganized ridges are a vivid point of identification. This trunk with its chaotic sculpturing is a mighty vault for wood that is among the hardest of our trees. Black locust wood is so tough that it almost never is used in sawed lumber, but is grabbed for fence posts, hubs of wheels, and railroad ties. To get a full-sized tie takes 45 years of growing. Our ancestors made wooden nails for ships and colonial houses of black locust. Today we make pins to hold the glass insulators of telephone wires, one of today's great uses for wood that can withstand weather and friction. As firewood, black locust is beautiful and unusual, although hard to start. Burns like coal, with bright-blue, concentrated flame almost like acetylene torch.

The flowers, like the leaves, are another contradiction of this scarred and heavy-wooded tree. In early summer black locust produces quantities of white sweet peas, with a delicate fragrance that permeates the air. The tree belongs to the same family as the sweet pea, and produces pods which may be seen hanging on the tree all winter. These are flat, 3 inches long, rich leathery brown, almost black. Open one, see the glistening white inside.

Black locust was almost blotted out by the Ice Age; the tree survived on earth only in a narrow oval in the southern Appalachian valleys. In our time it spreads with almost weed-like vitality, and you can see it in every state east of the Mississippi except Florida. Much of this is due to early settlers planting the tree for the beauty of its foliage and flowers, which make their remarkable contribution to the glory of the landscape after the tree has stood long months as an ungainly skeleton.

Robinia Pseudo-Acacia

Curling
pods of
Honey Locust

Honey Locust is one of the most remarkable trees of our land. Leaves are double multiple with small leaflets that give a tropical airy-fairy lightness to the foliage. Bark has a rough-smooth aspect, as though very rough bark had been smoothed with a trowel. Tree is detected quickly by long 10 inch pods. These are artfully twisted so they roll when tossed off the tree in a wind, providing a peculiar kind of seed dissemination. A jelly substance around the seeds in the beans is sweet, good to eat like honey. Even when pod is dry, the seeds can be sucked for the sweetness.

Honey locust has terrifying thorns in fantastic clusters. These are formed as single 4-inch needles and also as three-pronged daggers. These thorns are actually branches emerging from their own buds, as contrasted with tree thorns that are superficial prickles on the bark. A thornless variety is often planted in city parks. Biggest honey locusts are in southern Illinois, but tree extends all over West, flourishes in hot, sunny, dry ground. Much seen in South Dakota.

Gleditsia triacanthos

Honey Locust

THE BIRCHES_____

***Paper Birch** is so unlike any other tree that everyone knows it. It's the picture-book tree. The graceful white trunk beside blue waters, the bright green leaves have been seen in paintings and photographs by far more people than have ever seen the tree itself. It is a northern tree, not even getting as far down as New York City, except on mountains. In New England the paper birch is common in the hills, and graceful clumps lean beside the shores of lakes. It's usually part of the picture where people are skiing.

Paper birch is well named because bark can be peeled off in sheets of foolscap on which you can write. This sheet is chalky-white outside and golden-brown on the under surface. Where it has been peeled you see the orange inner bark, and white bark never grows again on that spot. Although soft and smooth to the touch, this is one of the most durable of plant substances. One birch log was buried so long in Siberia that the wood turned to stone, while the fossil log still wore its birch bark unchanged through centuries. Thoroughly waterproof, birchbark ca-

Paper Birch
leaves and tassels

53

noes made the American Indian famous.

If the artists hadn't claimed paper birch first, the engineers would have discovered it. Wearing this extraordinary bark, paper birch braves the blizzards right up to the Arctic Circle. Here is a fine example of cork insulation: a laminated (thin layer upon layer) skin of cork is built upon the tree. The cells have air spaces which give protection against sun and frost. Whiteness turns away the over-bright sun (most thin barked trees are very sensitive to intense light), and the corky, air-filled layers insulate the living cells just beneath the bark from the fierce deep-freeze of the North. Moreover, the slenderness of the trunk offers slight interference to high winds, and birch wood is springy. The tree will bow over and whip around, but recover serenely when the punishment is finished. It is this tough, elastic quality that makes birch ideal as a whipping rod—one way in which pioneer boys learned to know the name of the tree. Smooth and soft, this wood doesn't chafe fingers of symphony conductors who like their batons made of birch.

There are two white-barked birches, paper and gray. Both are important and distinctive, both are loosely called white birch.   *Betula papyrifera*

Gray Birch grows like a weed around cities. It is one of the commonest trees in greater New York. Southward it grows on unfertile land around Washington, Baltimore, and Philadelphia. Under these conditions, where most people catch

Gray Birch leaves
and tassels

sight of it, the bark is gray-white, often yellowish or dull. It bears many black marks, especially the conspicuous black triangles where old limbs broke off.

But also, gray birch goes northward where its bark is whiter, and it sets up an imitation of paper birch. To tell these two vivid trees apart, note how gray birch bark is silvery, not snowy white; also it is tighter and does not peel off in wide strips. If you're still not sure, look at the leaves; find them on the ground in winter. The gray birch leaf is a triangle with double teeth. The sides of the triangle tend to curve inward, narrowing the leaf and giving it a long, sharp point. The paper birch leaf is less angular, broader, and with a more rounded base.

Betula populifolia

★**Yellow Birch** has gold-and-silver curls all over its bark. These are thin, translucent, glistening with highlights. Best time to see this effect is in winter when the trunk is lighted by sunlight or snow. Take a curl of yellow birch bark in your hand, see how it shimmers silvery or golden. Yellow birch is a woods tree, it needs the moisture of shadows. In Appalachian and New England hills it is abundant around ravines with hemlock and moosewood. Bark curls are inflammable, make good tinder for starting a campfire even on a rainy day (be cautious!). Big, visible roots of yellow birch lay hold of rocky hillside like monstrous claws, or flow down from an old stump where a yellow birch seedling sprouted, then along the ground like serpents until

Yellow Birch and Sweet Birch leaves are similar.

they plunge into a pocket of soft humus. Twigs have mild wintergreen flavor not as strong as sweet birch. This is a rewarding tree to see on a hike or ride through the hills.

Betula lutea

Sweet Birch (also called black birch, cherry birch) is the wintergreen tree. On young trees, smooth, glossy, dark brown bark is peppered with white dashes. You might mistake it for a cherry tree until you taste the strong wintergreen flavor of twigs or buds. This is a commercial source of wintergreen oil. Sweet birch, as well as yellow birch, holds its seed tassels all winter, scattering tiny winged seeds conspicuously on the snow where they are important food for birds. The March wind litters the snow with these birch seeds in maple sugar season in northern New England woods. Sweet birch heartwood is brown with red tinge, takes fine polish, and is often used as imitation mahogany in furniture and boat trim.

Betula lenta

THE POPLARS_____

Poplars are fast-growing, gay trees with leaves that quiver. As a national asset they start rebuilding the woods fast after a fire. Poplar seeds germinate with alacrity in a burned place; little poplar trees make a cool, moist shadow for sprouting seeds of hemlock, oak, beech.

Poplar wood is soft and weak for construction. But its rate of growth keeps a good supply of wood coming for excelsior, match sticks, book paper. Also poplar wood holds nails firmly and offers clean, smooth surface for stenciling and labeling, making good crates and shipping boxes.

The name poplar brackets two other names—aspen and cottonwood. You can see the difference in these two kinds of poplars in the smooth, light green or whitish bark of aspen, compared to the deeply furrowed gray bark of cottonwood.

Trembling Aspen is a bright tree—bark is smooth, light olive green and foliage lighter green than the trees around. Leaves quiver like sparkling water, twinkling with the highlights of the sun and their lighter undersides. This is the only tree which can be identified by the way it moves. Other trees may wait for your close inspec-

tion, but the wonderful trembling aspen attracts the eye
with its fluttering hello.

This is the only transcontinental broadleaf tree; no
other grows naturally from Maine to California. It takes
its stand in conspicuous places, at the front of the woods
in full sunlight. It likes hillsides. This is the common aspen
of the northland. You see it around cabins and lakes of
canoe country. The straight trunk of young aspen with
smooth olive-green bark is a color note as vivid as birch.
An Indian name for it, "noisy leaf," translates the shimmering motion from the eyes to the ears.

Trembling aspen also has eye-filling details. Buds are
a polished red-brown, sharply pointed, twisted like a
small cornucopia that lies snugly against the twig. Other
trees have more formal or decorative buds, but poplar
buds have flair and vitality with a feeling of freedom and
energy that's good to share.

Trembling aspen leaf is small, almost round. Look well
at its stem; this is the most characteristic detail of the
tree. Whereas most leaf stems are merely stiff attach-
ments, this one is soft, flexible, and flat. The leaf dangles
on a ribbon set at right angles to the leaf blade. This
makes the whole thing wiggle in the slightest breeze.

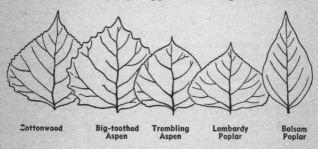

Cottonwood   Big-toothed   Trembling   Lombardy   Balsam
                   Aspen   Aspen   Poplar   Poplar

The tassels poured forth by this tree in April have given it the name of necklace tree in some places. These are the flowers (catkins). Aspen separates the sexes, as do ash and holly; thus one trembling aspen produces tassels with gorgeous deep-red stamens, while another one bears cottony tassels with seeds. Both kinds, cast off, cover the ground under their trees in spring, and are a sight to behold. *Populus tremuloides*

Bigtooth Aspen has a bit of leaf magic. At first leaves are like flannel, and densely white and woolly on under sides. Later they turn thin, green, and flutter like other poplar leaves. They have irregular, unusual scallops. Always you can tell the bigtooth by the big teeth on leaf edges. Otherwise it's hard to tell this tree from trembling aspen, except for an over-all feel. It grows in a lower, moister place, while trembling aspen usually stands on the hill. It is a larger tree, and young branches are brighter gray or yellow while trembling aspen's are red-brown. Plenty of both these trees around, compare these two common aspens and you'll find yourself reading trees. *Populus grandidentata*

Balsam Poplar (also wrongly called balm of Gilead) has the exception to the flat, flexible leaf stems of poplars. Stem is round; egg-shaped leaf does not flutter. This common poplar of Alaska, Labrador, North Canada, crosses our border into Maine and grows transcontinentally in Minnesota, North Dakota, and the northern Rocky Mountains. Buds in winter resist big freeze with heavy, glistening coating of resin, delightfully fragrant, sticky. *Populus Tacamahacca*

White Poplar

★Cottonwood is as familiar as the family dog. It is the usual, often the only tree over more space across these United States than any other one in our book. It takes in stride searing winds, drought, blazing sun, sudden sub-zero nights—and cheerily bobs up as the fastest-growing tree in the place. Cottonwood leaf with broad base is the outline of the pyramids of Egypt; right-angled teeth the stone steps.

Leaves begin dropping in mid-summer on top of the cotton tassels that whiten the ground. Thus cottonwood lays a soft rug where it's often too dry to grow grass.

This is the common tree in the 25 thousand miles of prairie shelter belts that airplane travelers see. Like willow, it can be grown from a fresh, green twig thrust in moist ground.   *Populus deltoides*

Lombardy Poplar is the sharply narrow oval pointing to the sky like a church steeple. It is famous in pictures of roads of France. With a form so striking we forget to look at the leaves, but you'll find a geometric figure of a broad triangle with baseline at right angles to the stem. Planted from Maine to Oregon. *Populus nigra var. italica*

Most Poplar leaves join ribbon-stem at right angles.

White Poplar is the peculiar tree with leaves snow-white and woolly below and dark green above, planted so much in parks and cemeteries. The "black and white" leaves vary in shape but suggest small maple leaves. The astonishing white wool creeps onto twigs and buds but rubs off nicely if you want to polish them up.   *Populus alba*

THE WILLOWS

***Black Willow** is the wide, ragged tree of the countryside. You see its heavy trunk, often two or more together, leaning over water from the bank of a stream or pond. It grows in rows along wet banks. Twigs spray out in large numbers from angles or knots in the trunk.

The bark of an old willow is heavily treaded and is often swirled and distorted, giving it a rugged grandeur all its own. However, this trunk is willow's only pretense at being a monarch. The wood is soft and almost useless for timber. Its twigs, called osiers, are woven into baskets and wicker furniture. Buds are smooth and dainty without overlapping scales, resembling bits of red sealing wax pressed between thumb and finger to flatten them against the twig. The mighty trunk supports a crown that is surprisingly light and delicate. Twigs are long and brittle, often so weak and flexible that they dangle, and from them swing leaves that are only 1½ inch wide and 5 inches long. These strangely narrow leaves taper sharply and have small, sharp teeth along the edge, like those of a fine saw. Two little sickle-shaped leaves circle the stem below the main leaf. These twin circular leaves are one of those surprising details you discover when you explore a tree.

Black Willow

Next to the fact that willow grows in wet places, its most conspicuous feature is the yellowness of the twigs. In winter these polished twigs catch the sun's rays and hold them with colorful effect of yellow against blue sky. The only tree which rivals willow with the winter color of its twigs is the poplar. However, poplar twigs are a dull, deep orange color, compared to the gold of willow. These twigs are not only the most conspicuous but also the most animated part of a willow. They behave like seeds in the way they reproduce the tree. Put a live willow twig into a glass of water and in a few days roots will grow out of one end and leaves out of the other. All it takes to plant a willow tree is to thrust one of these twigs into moist ground. The tree casts off its twigs the way other trees cast off their fruits.

The reason there are so many willows along so many streams in every part of our country is that one will lean over the water and drop twigs; these ride on the water and take root where they lodge in moist earth.

Salix nigra

Weeping Willow (who doesn't know it?) was planted by original settlers from Europe. It is like black willow except that the twigs are longer and dangle downward, sweeping the ground beneath the tree. Weeping willow is so distinctive that it is a landscape feature as a single specimen in a moist meadow, in a cemetery, or with a superb reflection in a park lake. Compare this willow's weeping habit with another planted tree—the Lombardy poplar which grows exactly to the contrary, shooting twigs upward. This willow makes a tree shower instead of a tower.

Salix babylonica

For willow and cottonwood of the West see pages 191-192.

THE UNDERSTORY TREES___

It is a healthy sign when you see little trees under big trees. The next generation is growing up. They offer you the best chance to reach out and touch leaves and buds, and you compare the roughness of elm leaf with the softness of walnut, the broad, black ash bud with the needle-sharp beech. Once you have held and stared at the crimson red maple bud, you will never again feel indifferent to buds. In addition, hidden in the camouflage of the understory are trees most people don't know. They usually have slender trunks that bend and run out toward the nearest space with the most light. Formless, according to the standard idea of what a tree should look like, these little trees of the shadows have marvelous art in their details, and extraordinary fruits:

★Sassafras is famous for its three shapes of leaf on the same branch. This trick starts off tree exploring with a bang. If you have an artist's eye, you will be even more delighted with the green tone of the leaf. Its richness is enhanced because there are no highlights. This tree

**Blue Sassafras
fruits sit on
coral stems.**

grows in mottled shadows which mellow the beautiful suede green. If you could reproduce this wonderful green in home decorating, it would be deeply satisfying.

A positive check on sassafras is the flavor of its twigs. Twigs are bright green near their tips and turn up gracefully. Chew this —you taste spicy, aromatic oil not to be described in words. Sweet birch twig is wintergreen, cherry is bitter, spice bush is cinnamon, sassafras is sassafras. For a totally different flavor than the one used for sassafras tea (made from the roots) and gumdrops, the leaves are dried and powdered and a few spoonfuls added at the last minute to a kettle of gumbo soup for excellent flavor and thickening. Only the South's Creoles make the real thing.

Typically American, sassafras grows nowhere else in the world except southeast Asia. All over our eastern states it's common both as an understory tree and also in dry, sandy spots along roadsides. Southward, it achieves 50 feet, with deeply furrowed bark that creates an illusion of great age.

Yellow-green flowers in early spring are conspicuous. More thrilling is the huge caterpillar that fills his body

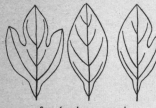

**Sassafras leaves come in
three shapes.**

with translucent green fluid from the sassafras leaf where he feeds. A black spot looks like a fierce cyclops' eye at the tip of his nose. He's harmless and will turn into one of our most beautiful butterflies—

Sunlight on paper birch traces the brightest tree etching of the winter woods.

Tall crowns of scattered pines against clouds are a pageant of the South.

American elms accent the colonial atmosphere of Williamsburg, Va.

Trees and flowers make New England roadsides the gayest of our country.

Contrasting forms of red cedar and elm combine with a Pennsylvania cottage to design a winter picture.

Black walnut's long limbs reach far out.
(The New York Botanical Garden)

Pin oak's finespun branches plunge down.
(Near Richmond, Va.)

Apple blossoms flash below a stately elm at Lime Rock, Conn.

The swaying of weeping willow's flexible branches is a remarkable tree motion. (The James River at Berkeley Manor, Va.)

Elms and maples give New England towns the settlers' touch. (Salisbury, Conn.)

the swallowtail.

Sassafras variifolium

Witch Hazel shoots its seeds through the woods. Flower (above) blossoms in fall.

★**Witch Hazel,** unlike other trees, flowers in the fall when tiny yellow ribbons dangle all over it. Often these petals curl and hang on all winter. In New England witch hazel is a large shrub, becoming a tree in the Carolina and Tennessee mountains. The leaf has eccentric charm. Margins ripple smoothly while the whole leaf is thrown off-center as though by a steady breeze blowing across it.

Witch hazel packs its biggest surprise in the pop guns scattered over its twigs. These are tough, powerful seedcases, each holding two tiny black footballs. When cold dries this contraption in the fall, it opens like a bird's mouth and shoots out the seeds some 10 feet into the woods. Witch hazel bark, distilled, makes a solution that smells delicious, feels so clean you find it on drugstore shelves—try it for mosquito bites. *Hamamelis virginiana*

Hop Hornbeam (also called ironwood) growing slowly in the shadows builds such hard wood it burns like anthracite. This makes a good mallet handle, or rake teeth, but it's hard to whittle. The best identification is the fruit. These resemble oval paper bags, each of which contains one seed; unusual, for most fruits have numbers of seeds. These paper bags overlap and dangle in a loose cone-like cluster. Leaves are flannel soft,

Witch Hazel

Hop Hornbeam

with fine sharp teeth—really exquisite, but it takes scrutiny to appreciate them, as they superficially look like birch leaves. Bark is shredded with narrow gray strips. Easily confused with other trees; you know it first by spotting the unique fruit, then fitting it together with leaves and bark—hop hornbeam is worth knowing. Grows in dry woodsy places from Maine to Texas. *Ostrya virginiana*

Cluster of Hop Hornbeams paper-bag fruits

Blue Beech seed attached to graceful wing

Blue Beech (also called American hornbeam) has a trunk with muscular ridges like a man's forearm when he clenches his fist. Bark is smooth, blue-gray. Wood is hard like hop-hornbeam, but trunk is too slender to be useful. This tough little tree dangles clusters of nuts, each fixed to an ornate wing shaped like a narrow maple leaf. Blue beech is said to be "shapeless;" actually it is dynamically formed, shaped by light, its muscular trunk and wiry twigs reaching for the sun. You find it along woodland streams, and in wet places from Maine to Texas. *Carpinus caroliniana*

THE BIG
FLOWERING TREES_____

What is your power of observation? If good, then you can enjoy many kinds of beautiful flowers on trees, such as elm which bears a crown of dark purple gauze in early spring before leaves are out. Red maple flowers are rich red, conspicuous against blue sky. Norway maple has bright yellow-green flowers. Sassafras has compact bunches of yellow flowers. Basswood, after the leaves are out, is loaded with cream-white flowers.

A few large trees have flowers so vivid that when they are out, they arrest attention even when you aren't looking for them. Flowers are their best identification.

See also black locust, magnolia, tulip, sorrel, black cherry, horse chestnut.

Catalpa (also called Indian-bean) is the front page tree. Everything about it is interesting. Any time of year, find the nearest catalpa and it gives you something you can't forget. In late June flowers pile up all over the tree in ten-inch mounds. Petals are scalloped and ruffled, mostly white, but with brown or purple spots and two

**Pod and leaf of
Catalpa**

gold stripes. These lines point toward the nectar well, so that a bumblebee knows the way.

Leaves are big hearts. They have a basic simplicity the way a child might draw them with broad strokes. Compare these with the round, gay little heart-leaves of redbud. Catalpa leaves, strangely, secrete nectar, as do flowers. Notice the nectar glands at the base of stem.

Pods stream down in large numbers, hanging on most of the winter. Although from a little distance they resemble giant string beans, these are not true beans, but long, tough seed cases, round and slender as a panatella cigar. Catalpa seeds released the following spring are equally strange—out of its string bean pod come papery flakes an inch long with silver fringe at each end.

In winter, the tree is stiff, dead looking. But the awkward branches have marks on them by which you can identify catalpa instantly. They are oval scars on raised bases. They go round the stem in whorls of three, one

Catalpa flowers

little scar and two big ones. As they mark the places where leaves fell off, it follows that catalpa leaves grow in whorls of three around a branch.

For a tree that grows so fast that it can add an inch wide ring to its wood in a year, the wood is surprisingly durable. Railroads *Catalpa bignonioides* make ties of catalpa.

Paulownia (also called empress tree) is the fastest growing commercial wood tree in America. In a single year a seedling may rise 20 feet. Ailanthus and sumac compete in speed of elongating, but these are weed trees with pithy wood, while paulownia's wood has commercial value.

Paulownia leaf (above) is less pointed at tip, has bigger stem than Catalpa.

Paulownia is a medium-sized, beautiful shade tree with enormous leaves, often seen in parks, on streets, college grounds in eastern United States, especially around Philadelphia, Baltimore, Washington. This is one of the American settler trees, brought from the Orient during the past century, which escaped from cultivation and became part of our land. Others are ailanthus, mulberry, weeping willow, ginkgo.

People who know the big, light green leaves of catalpa often mistake paulownia for that tree. But paulownia flowers are light purple—catalpa, white. When leaves are off, paulownia arouses curiosity by conspicuous fruits unlike any other tree's. People say, "What is that tree with the large clusters of grapes?"

These fruits are oval, the size of a healthy pecan nut. They are startling in their reproductive power—each contains 2 thousand little winged seeds. If you count the fruits on a lusty paulownia, you can figure that a single tree produces 21 million seeds. No wonder foresters are eyeing this tree. It grows in almost any soil—in Washington, D. C., one achieved three feet from a seed

Paulownia pods

that landed in mortar between bricks of a wall. Paulownia can build sawlogs fast. Extra light weight but strong for crates and boxes in air express, where weight counts.   *Paulownia tomentosa*

Horse-Chestnut from the Balkans is at home in America as much as a tree can be. Ever since Longfellow's village blacksmith made his anvil clang under this "spreading chestnut," people in eastern states have planted it around home. Take a drive in late May and someone in the car is sure to cry out about the tall, heavily leafed dome with candelabra of white flowers scattered all over it. These have yellow and red spots, and long yellow stamens that protrude far out of the flower tube.

There's no excuse to think this a catalpa because of the flowers. It blooms a month earlier, but glance at the leaves. Five, sometimes seven, big, wedge-shaped leaflets fan out like the fingers of your hand. Leaf opens like an umbrella. At first the leaflets are turned down, then in a single day they lift, broaden out, and the tree seems covered with countless little whirling helicopters.

Lower branches curve up and down and up again like a roller coaster. At twig tip is a huge bud. Look for this; it glistens with resin as though just varnished.

Horse-chestnut is elaborate but mussy. Flowers fall off, litter the lawn. Fruits keep dropping. They are exceedingly prickly; nobody goes barefoot under a horse-chest-

Horse Chestnut

nut. When leaves fall, they come all apart so that leaflets and stems flutter down separately. The seed is a beautiful brown leather ball with a gray eye. It's bitter, narcotic, only fit for horses they used to say, and that's how the tree gets its name. *Aesculus hippocastanum*

Buckeye is scattered around the Middle West. * Comments on horse-chestnut apply to this tree. Differences are incidental but clear, and of interest to tree detectives: flowers are pale yellow, instead of white. Leaflets are narrower, smaller. Big bud is dull, smooth, not glistening with varnish. Crushed leaves and bark have a rank odor to sniff for identification, otherwise to shun. Buckeye wood is light, springy, hard to split, is used for artificial limbs. *Aesculus glabra*

*Ohio's tree-conscious, strong-arm settlers, carving out their homeland with gun and axe, admired the flowers and leaves of this tree, built their homes beside it. They coined its lusty name which rolls so smoothly off the tongue that Ohio is proud to be called the Buckeye State.

THE LITTLE
FLOWERING TREES_____

These are like play-things compared to the big trees, and are often no taller than the ceiling of your room. The trunks are usually slender, inconspicuous, and lean a little in support of compact, round heads, which flare in springtime as though bright white or purple-pink parasols had opened suddenly in the sunlight. Many people see these trees who ordinarily pay little heed to trees. But in May, when people rush out into the country, dogwood, cherry, red-bud, shadblow are startlingly vivid. Moreover, you see little flowering trees: magnolia, crab-apple, cherry, haw-thorn, cultivated for their flowers in city parks, yards, and gardens. Certain little flowering trees are ideal for streets and corners of big, modern cities; they fit into small space, producing blooms even in light reflected from walls of buildings. As the big shade trees of the horse and buggy era vanish from downtown streets and squares, the little flowering trees can bring back a value lost from the heart of the city.

★**Redbud** (also called Judas tree) is the only wild American tree with bright purple-red flowers. Riding in

mid-spring (same as dogwood time) in
Pennsylvania, Ohio, and southward,
you'll see redbud with hackberry, oak,
walnut, hemlock in hilly places, and
often only a single tree blazing on a hillside pasture. In peach-tree land (Georgia, Alabama, the Carolinas) redbud, at
a distance, could be mistaken for a peach

Redbud pods

tree in bloom, or a purple flowering crab. But these fruit
trees are cultivated, while redbud is the colorful doll of
our hardwood forest. Its bright, garish purple does not
look well with blue sky, but redbud is effective because
it is small and usually overtopped by other broadleaf
trees, evergreens, and shadows.

Flowers cover the tree, springing out from twigs, main
branches and even from the trunk, whereas most tree
flowers bloom from the tips of twigs. Redbud flowers are like sweet-peas, and whirling around their stems they resemble little
dancing shoes.

If redbud didn't put on such a brilliant
show of flowers it might be famous for its
leaves. These are round hearts; press some
for Valentine's Day. Pods also are a feature.
Shaped like ordinary pea pods, these are
rose colored. Buds are purple-red, as the name of the tree
implies, but they're only ⅛ inch and hard to see. It's an exciting little tree. *Cercis canadensis*

Redbud leaf is a
perfect heart.

★**Flowering Dogwood** is America's most decorative tree
and enjoys among trees the same reputation as the robin
among birds. Dogwood chooses the week in the year when

it will be most conspicuous before leaves come out on surrounding trees to unroll broad white blossoms in the sunlight. Each is a masterpiece of design, like an ivory Maltese cross. All the flowers on the tree unroll at the same time and are extended in layers with shadowy spaces between the blossoms that accentuate this effect. This makes a mosaic that people strive to reproduce on draperies and wallpaper. Examine the twigs that support this mosaic and you will see how gracefully they curve to form the planes. Each flower is held at right angles to the direction of brightest light, giving it maximum exposure. Thus in the open the dogwood covers itself with an umbrella of flowers shaped by the dome of sky. On the edge of the woods it will hold its mosaic toward the parkway, where the motorist catches the effect even at fifty miles an hour.

The dogwood is a small tree, so that in the woods it is part of the understory, along with cherry, shadblow and redbud that bloom about the same time. In the midst of the woods the dogwood marquee is spread low among the tall, sunlit tree trunks. This is one of the most unusual effects of the spring woods, but you have to get out of the city to see it.

Dogwood

To understand this tree, mark it when the flowers are out so as to find it in the winter when it seems to have disappeared. You'll see the flower buds held up at the twig tips as though the tree were offering a toast to the woods with a thousand tiny silver goblets. Peer closely, note the four bud divisions. The sealing material between them will melt, the four segments will lift and re-

volve outward, exposing their white inner surfaces. Each part elongates from
the base, as fingernails grow, and not the
tips. What were bud scales now turn into
what look like broad white petals. On
most trees bud scales fall off when buds
open, but the flowering dogwood con-
verts them into the most conspicuous
part of the flower.

Silvery Dogwood
bud can be seen in
fall and winter.

In the northern part of its range, New York and New
England, the flowers are white as snow; they turn to
waxy white and light greenish white as they move southward. Near Lancaster, Ohio, grows a dog-
wood that produces pink blossoms which
provides nurserymen with grafts to raise
"red flowering dogwood".

Red chemicals are hidden in this tree. Its
berries are shiny red footballs ½ inch long,
Its fall foliage, too, is deep red.

Flowering dogwood is hard but doesn't
weather well, so no mill thirsts for it. Once
upon a time spear shafts were made of it,
and recently shafts of golf clubs.

Dogwood blossoms

Cornus florida

Shadblow (also called serviceberry) is like a puff of
white steam in the early spring woods. The white flowers
may appear at the top of a slender trunk that reaches
high, for a little tree, but gets up only to the mezzanine
of a tall woods. Shadblow is often a shrub, in New
England,* where you see it on the edge of the woods
or scattered around pastures. The very earliness of its

---

*Between Boston and Providence low pastures are white with it in April.
But the typical place is the high, hilly woods.

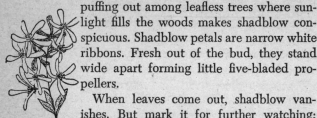

puffing out among leafless trees where sunlight fills the woods makes shadblow conspicuous. Shadblow petals are narrow white ribbons. Fresh out of the bud, they stand wide apart forming little five-bladed propellers.

Shadblow

When leaves come out, shadblow vanishes. But mark it for further watching; you'll be rewarded. Bark is smooth, feels good to touch, looks rich and modern like bark of blue beech. Fruit is a tiny, dark blue apple, delicious to eat except that it isn't big enough to sink your teeth in. Some of our best-known birds: flicker, cardinal, bluebird, cedar waxwing, robin, frantically snatch these half-inch apples off the tree as soon as they are ripe——one reason why you can't have a bowl of

Shadblow

them on your table. The shadblow bud has long, red-brown scales edged with silver hairs that tend to twist like a living flame at the tip of the twig. Its flare and beauty is unsurpassed in tree buds.

Amelanchier canadensis

Hawthorn is eccentric in both appearance and behavior. Zigzag branches stab out horizontally. Leaves have sharp, irregular teeth. Hawthorn bears white roses in June and in the fall tiny red apples that hang on all winter. Rose, apple, and hawthorn all belong to the same family.

Hawthorn is encountered in rough, rocky fields or near brooks, and is known by its long, straight, exceedingly sharp thorns in the impenetrable tangle of branches. Honey locust and osage orange also bear vicious thorns but are so different in form, leaves and fruit that there is no confusion with hawthorn. This is the only heavily thorned tree with sharply toothed, single leaves.

When men cleared the land and laid the axe to forest trees, hawthorn woke up and evolved so many new species even experts can't keep track of them. Gray's Manual lists 180 kinds. They invade pastures and are a pesky nuisance to the farmer, although picturesque to the artist. A slow-growing tree with tough wood and roses for flowers can hardly be termed a weed. Moreover, birds love to build their nests in hawthorn for the armor gives protection from cats, children, squirrels, hawks. Hawthorns are citadels for goldfinch, cardinal, cedar waxwing, robin. Here are the hawthorns you are most likely to see:

1. Cockspur Thorn, long daggers up to 8 inches shoot out from above little oblong leaves. *Crataegus crus-galli*

2. White Thorn, frequent in old pasture fields. Small, so you can look right over the top. Intricate branches conceal song sparrow nests. Almost thornless compared to the others. *Crataegus intricata*

Cockspur
Thorn

English Hawthorn

3. Washington Thorn, taller, southerly, but common around Washington D. C. Superabundance of flowers, and bright red fruits attract the eye all winter. Filled with slender exceedingly sharp 2 inch thorns.

Crataegus Phaenopyrum

4. English Hawthorn, best-known park and garden kind. Varieties with white, pink or red double flowers. Leaves fancy with three lobes. Strong 1 inch thorns. All over England in hedges that have made literature.

Crataegus Oxyacantha

Yellowwood (also called virgilia) is so interesting you should ask your park commissioner or botanical garden where you can see it. Discovered on limestone cliffs in Kentucky and Tennessee, this tree is now planted as far north as Boston, and Cleveland is raising a great number for street trees. Leaves are silver velvet in spring and turn clear yellow in fall. Fragrant white flowers of a large sweetpea type spout out from the ends of twigs in early summer, bending them over with their weight so that clusters dangle like wisteria and the tree buzzes with

Yellowwood

bees. These flowers are a special event because they may skip a year or two, but, even without flowers, yellowwood is a healthy tree with attractive foliage. Bark is silvery smooth like beech. Wood is hard, bright yellow, takes a beautiful polish, but is seldom used for furniture or interior trim due to the rareness of the tree in forests and the slenderness of its trunk. The name "virgilia" is pleasant to remember. *Cladrastis lutea*

Mountain Ash takes first prize for producing the most brilliant fruit of any of our trees. This little tree of rocky places, where cold spring water moistens the roots, is laden in fall with massive clusters of orange-red fruits. They are like tiny pears and so bitter no one eats them. Even birds turn away, eating them only as emergency rations. The eye appeal is so great that if you travel in northern places—hilltops in New England, cool shores of Lake Superior and Huron, you will be thrilled by the sight of this tree. White flowers in flat-topped clusters festoon it in early summer, but these flowers get scant attention because the intense fruits steal the show. Don't miss the leaves; they are like ferns up to ten inches long with artistic saw-edged leaflets.

Not a relative of the true ash, mountain ash is akin to the apple tree, but resembles nothing but itself.

Sorbus americana

European Mountain Ash is from the highlands of Scotland, has similar leaves but is weighted with even larger fruits. Planted in parks and yards.   *Sorbus aucuparia*

Hercules' Club (also called devil's walking stick) has the biggest multiple leaves of any tree in the U.S.A.: 3 feet long, 2 wide. These are compounded of a double series of small leaflets so you get no impression of big leaves at first glance. Hercules' club looks like nothing else in our treedom. Trunk is a pole six inches thick, rising 20 feet or so unbranched, often with several poles growing in a clump. The big leaves gush out from peak of pole, falling by their weight into form of broad umbrella. Skin-tearing prickles are scattered over bark so boys never shinny up this pole. Effect is that of a small royal palm; foliage has tropical luxuriance. Unfolding leaves are bronze colored and turn bronze-red mottled with yellow in fall.

Creamy white flower clusters mount like geysers four feet above leaf tops. Berries resemble little white ivory billiard balls, ripening to blue, devoured by bluebirds and blue jays.

This peculiar tree grows in warm nooks at edge of woods from Pennsylvania to Missouri, southward. In the South it grows up to 50 feet.   *Aralia spinosa*

If you explore the mountains of Tennessee and North Carolina, you may discover two little trees loaded with white flowers as though a landscape gardener had gone

Hercules' Club—largest
multiple leaf

into a ravine to plant them. But you may see them more easily in parks, gardens and lawns up north. Both trees are slender with plain oval leaves. Only the flowers stop you; otherwise you may as well skip these trees:

Silverbell Tree has elegant snow-white bells pendant all over tree appearing same time dogwood and redbud are in bloom. Each is shaped like a snowdrop flower of a late winter lawn.

Halesia carolina

Silverbell blossoms

Fringe Tree gives gay, fringy effect with delicate buff-white clusters of flowers. Oval leaves are in pairs, have smooth edges. It flowers in early summer after lilacs are through. An old-fashioned tree decoration that goes with southern colonial homes. Fruit is like small purple plum.

Chionanthus virginicus

Fringe tree flowers

THE FRUIT TREES_____

★**Apple** tree stands in the same relationship to man as the dog. There leans the apple by the old American homestead. It was tamed from wild trees before written history and has lived with us sociably ever since. It has a short, muscular trunk, steel-gray bark with wide, round ridges that spiral as though the whole tree, twisted by wind, had spun around a little. It offers a wide umbrella for cool shade on a hot day. It declares the climax of spring with its white fragrant flowers. It sends a boy back to school in the fall with a mouthful of crackling, juicy fruit.

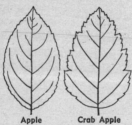

Apple   Crab Apple

Flowers and fruit are so diverting we forget to see the apple tree closely. Many twigs fail to shoot out in length—they are stubby, thick, like a short segment of a compressed screen door spring. Each lumpy segment, a fraction of an inch in length, is a year's growth. There is singular fitness in this. A good apple is heavy, it is a beautiful porous ball 85 per cent water. If apples were carried on ordinary long slender twigs, they might bang together and be bruised in a high wind. The strong rigid spurs bear the load with safety and economy.

Good eating apples have names such as Baldwin, McIntosh, Delicious, Northern Spy, Pippin, Rhode Island Greening. Plant their seeds and you'll have a tree bearing small, sour apples. This mysterious fact shows how quickly a tame apple tree reverts to the wild state. Apples are held true to type through the equally mysterious fact that the fruit is constant in quality only if it is bred through wood instead of through seed. The original Baldwin tree was discovered in a fence corner at Lowell, Massachusetts, in 1793 by Mr. Baldwin. Since then, through grafting, millions of trees have produced Baldwin apples, all of them borne on the same stream of wood unbroken from that single, original tree. McIntosh, an Ontario farmer, over a century ago was alert enough to recognize good apples on a wild tree that started another stream of wood bearing the McIntosh apple down to us. Saw handles are made from apple wood, and it's excellent for whittling.   *Malus pumila*

Crab Apple is the little, stiff, crooked tree in the hedgerow or old pasture. It shows that animals are active and happy thereabouts; white-tailed deer, raccoon, skunk, fox go for the small acid apples and scatter the seeds. If people get there first, the result is clear, orange-red crabapple jelly. The small apples (1 inch in diameter) feel waxy to the touch, indicating lots of jelly-making substance in the skin.

With its low, wide top and crooked branches, often shrubby with several trunks, it looks like a crab walking across an old field, if you feel imaginative.

Crab flowers are pinker, more fragrant than the eating apple tree. Nurserymen sell imported types just for their showy flowers. The flowering apple tree you see in the park is apt to be a Siberian crab.   *Malus coronaria*

★**Black Cherry** is on the first team with the American hardwoods—growing all over eastern U. S. with elm, oak, maple, birch. It has so little outward distinction that few people recognize our only valuable cherry tree. Branches are often broken, dishevelled, and favorite pastures for tent caterpillars. Buds are inconspicuous; dark red, shiny. Leaves are stereotyped ovals. The bark of an old trunk is almost black, made of small broken pieces of the original smooth surface. But run your eye up to the top of trunk and limbs—you may see there the glossy, dark red cherry bark peppered with short horizontal lines.

Black Cherry leaf has incurving teeth.

The lines are breathing pores (lenticels) to let air inside the tree where the shoe-polished bark is air-proof. White flowers droop in clusters the size of your longest finger. Dark purple cherries, two months later, are seldom seen because some 70 kinds of birds go after them.

For sure identification chew the end of a twig, taste the peculiar cherrystone bitterness. Another detail to check is the unusual incurving of the teeth along leaf edge.

Early settlers cut big cherry trees for paneling and furniture, rivaling black walnut in beauty. Cherry wood grows richer, darker with age. They also made cherry bounce from fruits, though we wonder how the crop was picked before the birds took it. With scarcity of big trees, cherry wood today is used for small things where smooth perfection of wood with no warping is needed: spirit levels, saw handles, blocks for elec-trotypes. In a tough, scrubby form, black cherry is one of the commonest trees in woods around New York City.

Fruit of Black Cherry

Prunus serotina

Sweet Cherry is better recognized as cherry because the trunk keeps smooth, glossy, red-brown bark. Horizontal lines in the bark turn yellow and callous but they are vivid, decorative. Sweet cherry leaves have irregular teeth as contrasted with the even saw-teeth of black cherry. Old homestead property often has this cherry, and it escapes to the edge of the woods. It bears so many good eating cherries that people as well as birds can have some to eat. *Prunus avium*

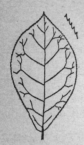

Chokecherry is a scraggly version of the wild black cherry. Its red-purple fruit puckers your mouth, but makes good pie. The fame of this tree is in the way it attracts birds. Twittering in the thickets is often caused by excitement over it. Dangling white fingers of flowers make this small rough tree with black bark conspicuous in the spring. Teeth of leaves point out, compared with incurved teeth of black cherry, twigs are as bitter to taste. One of the most widely distributed trees in North America.   *Prunus virginiana*

Chokecherry has tiny jagged teeth.

Wild Red Cherry (also called bird, pin, or fire cherry) has bright translucent red cherries on long stems, a few together in clumps instead of finger-like clusters. The red-brown bark is smooth and peels off. Grows in burnt-over places with aspen and gray birch.

Prunus pensylvanica

Peach is the first fruit tree to bloom in the spring. Rose-pink blossoms flare while rest of landscape is still drab. You can't miss this tree while motoring in March-April through Virginia and southward. Cherry, apple, and pear have white flowers. In size and color peach flowers look like redbud, but the latter blooms later, in the woodland, while peach is planted by a house or in an open field.

Prunus Persica

Other fruit trees planted for flowers in gardens and parks are oriental cherries (finest rose-colored, double-flowered display in America in Brooklyn Botanic Garden), plum, almond, prune, apricot.

CITY TREES_____

City people used to live with trees as easily as country people. They simply moved in elm, maple, linden, and so on. For a generation cities like Columbus, Ohio, would hardly be recognized without its elms—in that city four rows of elms stood along downtown Broad Street. The inexorable pressure of big buildings, crowds, automobiles has pushed trees out of the cities—except in parks. But a blank was left in people's lives—green is easy on the eyes, shade is comforting, buds are reassuring when they open in the spring. People have missed them and yearn for them.

Today city planners are searching for trees from a fresh viewpoint. The traditional shade trees are not coming back. How to make a tree grow in an intolerable situation? The problem: polluted air; desert aridity of pavements; salt used to melt snow and ice; visits of male dogs.

Certain trees resist city conditions better than others, for example, pin oak, catalpa, poplar, Norway maple will do business in crowded suburbs. Cleveland is experimenting with small flowering trees. In big downtown industrial cities the following three trees have supreme fortitude.

Ginkgo leaf

Ginkgo (also called maidenhair tree) should be exciting as a crocodile on a big city street. Yet millions in Washington, New York, Cincinnati, and other cities pass by without a glance because ginkgo seems like an ordinary tree. But its leaves are fern leaves, from the Age of Reptiles. A weird fact is that the pollen of this tree is unlike that of other trees of our day, but swims like fern sperms wriggling through rain or dew instead of being blown or transferred by insects. Science once tried to relate ginkgo to yew, a member of pine family, with berry-like fruit. Now a class of tree has been set up by botanists for the ginkgo alone. There is no other tree like it, delivered, as it were, by parcel post from the age of dinosaurs into the heart of our teeming cities.

See the little leaf fans with wavy edges and a slice like a thin piece of pie cut out. Fruits like tiny buff plums dangle on stems. Outer husk has foul smell; nut inside is shelled by pinching its thin coat, out pops silver-white kernel; nourishing, but tastes like rancid butter. Don't expect to find these fruits often. It takes 30 years to produce them. Most ginkgos are too young or else are male trees that have no berries.

Somehow ginkgo's peculiar leaves resist fumes and soot; somehow a tree evolved in a bygone age can take our ruthless cities, creating trunk, leaf and fruit from miserable dirt below the scorching pavements.

Ginkgo biloba

Ailanthus (also called tree of heaven) is the luxurious backyard tree you see over the city fence. Or if there is a square foot of soil facing a hot dirty street, ailanthus will grow as though in a cool, moist garden. City rubbish seems to make satisfactory fertilizer for a tree that has more virility than most weeds. Pith of twig is huge, bright orange, bark is decorated with big shield-shaped scars where branches used to be attached. Leaves are tropical ferns in aspect, spouting up gay, fresh green, but if you crush one, the odor is rank. Seeds are airplane propellers, two blades twisted, spinning the seed through the air when it lets go.   *Ailanthus altissima*

Ailanthus

Ailanthus seeds

London Plane Tree is like a sycamore with patches of yellow and brown on trunk, instead of white patches. Fruit balls dangle in twos from branches. This tree was bred by crossing two kinds of sycamores. It prospers downtown better than any other standard shade tree. New York City has many in midtown streets, as in front of Rockefeller Plaza, and it is doing a good job providing cool shade for bench-sitters in little park back of Public Library in heart of Manhattan.   *Platanus acerifolia*

THE MULBERRIES _____

Mulberry is an exciting little tree. The leaves suggest that evolution of the ages is going on before our eyes, but has not yet settled on a fixed mulberry leaf form. Although all leaves have sharp, irregular teeth with vivid veins sunk into them, some are oval, others have an eccentric lobe or two, like your thumb, or merely a lump. Others may have a number of lobes and turn into fancy designs. Sassafras leaves also come in a variety of shapes but have smooth edges.

White Mulberry is the kind usually seen planted around older towns of the East and sometimes along New England roads settled during the last century. It has a

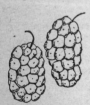
White Mulberry

short, leaning trunk and low, wide-spreading head casting dense shade; very inviting for a picnic on a hot day. Fruit is like white blackberries. These ripen a few at a time during several summer months instead of ripening and falling together like most tree fruits. People don't enjoy the taste but mulberries are a great attraction for birds, and good for fattening poultry.

This is the silkworm tree. American settlers, including George Washington and Benjamin Franklin, planted mulberry freely, hoping to start a silk industry. But, for Americans, it was too much work to pick and feed leaves to silkworms at just the right moment. The fastidious worm will only eat them slightly wilted, rejecting a fresh leaf or one that is badly wilted. It takes a ton of leaves to make a few pounds of raw silk. Cut a twig when sun is hot and see the milky sap ooze out, and you will see the chemical which is turned to silk threads by the worm.

Morus alba

Three kinds of White Mulberry leaves

Paper Mulberry is a true colonial landscape feature. Thousands of visitors marvel at this tree in Williamsburg, Jamestown, and the old Virginia estates. It's fairly common throughout the South. The characteristic that stops you is the trunk contorted with huge convolutions that seem to speak of great age. This is an abnormal growth common to this tree. Where the bark is normal it is smooth and yellowish, with dim lines interlacing like etching on a ground glass surface.   *Broussonetia papyrifera*

Red Mulberry is our native American tree that grows tall and straight in the southern Appalachian woods. You're not likely to see it. Middle Western and Southern farms seek it out for fence posts, for the wood is hard, tough, and doesn't decay on contact with soil.

This mulberry makes good shade tree to plant beside chicken yard where it drops fattening food all summer long that poultry love. Like all mulberries, sap is milky. This is family relative to tropical fig and rubber trees. Milky sap of the latter is latex for natural rubber.

Morus rubra

HACKBERRY

Hackberry is the unknown tree. Taking it for an elm, most people don't bother to look at it twice. In Middle West and South you can see many a hackberry with a tall, wide sweeping head that arouses curiosity in the way it reaches skyward so royally.

Around old southern plantation houses and campuses (for example, Hampton Institute, Virginia) the light gray bark catches the eye with its corky lumps.

Another peculiar way to spot hackberry is by dark clumps of twigs, called witches' brooms, high in the tree. A fungus disease stimulates these clumps. This mars the appearance of a fine tree, but it usually doesn't hurt its health, and makes a point of identification that can be seen from afar, especially in winter. Witches' brooms on hackberry can be confused with mistletoe, but the latter has evergreen leaves, while the witches' brooms are all twigs when the leaves are off.

Without corky lumps on the trunk and witches' brooms aloft (hackberry may lack these abnormalities), look for a peculiar detail seen when you split a twig lengthwise with a sharp pocket knife. The pith of most tree twigs is whitish or yellow in the center. Hackberry pith has a row of tiny white wax paper partitions close together but with air spaces between.

When leaves are out, you see wonderfully graceful leaf designs. One side has a wider sweep, making it lopsided like

Hackberry
leaf and seed

elm and basswood leaves. Hackberry, however, tapers exquisitely, forming a curve that is a segment of the dynamic spiral described by a clam shell, or a sandy beach curved by water currents, or an airplane in a sweeping turn.

This tree produces berries the size of peas dangling singly along a twig. When ripe, they are dark purple and sweet to eat. But birds usually get them first, and anyway the flesh is so thin you chew mostly on a hard seed.

Celtis occidentalis

Sugarberry, a southern hackberry, has narrower leaves, smaller berries, more warts on trunk, and is often used for a shady street tree, especially in New Orleans.

Celtis laevigata

SUMAC

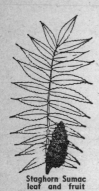

Staghorn Sumac is the small, rank tree that grows in clumps along roadsides and on rocky, sterile spots. Tropical, fern-like foliage is surmounted by crimson plush berries in dense rough pyramids. Clump is lemony to taste, helps quench thirst, makes good lemonade. Lush and colorful, and with red fall foliage, sumac is one of the features of our eastern landscapes. You'll know staghorn by dense, sticky hairs on berries and twigs. In winter, dark branches; angular, awkward, blunt, suggest hairy antlers of young stag. Wood is soft, milky, useless—but if you push out big orange pith you have a tube to blow through to make fire burn better.   *Rhus typhina*

Staghorn Sumac
leaf and fruit

Poison Sumac is more vicious than poison ivy. Know it to avoid. Signs are smooth-edged, graceful leaves on slender treelet in swampy place. October leaves are gorgeous flame color—look out—don't take any home! Berries dangle in loose cluster, waxy white, while berries of harmless sumac are red. Remember danger sign: white berries on pretty little tree in swampy place. *Rhus vernix*

Dwarf Sumac is commonest of this group. It grows on dry uplands and roadsides from Canada to Texas. Leaf stem has wings between pairs of leaflets. Berries are red, and plant is not poisonous. Usually a shrub.

Rhus copallina

THE EVERGREENS⸺⸺⸺⸺

The day you walk up to
an evergreen and say that it is a pine or spruce, or hemlock, and so on—that day you'll discover trees in a way
that brings pleasure wherever you go. Evergreens are to
be seen almost everywhere.

The needle is as true a leaf as a maple leaf, even though
it is exceedingly long and narrow. The cone is a peculiar
kind of fruit. Instead of juicy flesh or husk or seeds encased in various kinds of containers, the cone consists of
wooden discs on which seeds lie naked upon their upper
surfaces. The discs are folded up tight while their seeds
are ripening. Finally they swing wide open and winged
seeds fly away in the wind. The cone is, indeed, a silent,
efficient mechanism.

You can instantly tell six kinds of evergreen trees as
follows:

Pine: Long, flexible needles in a bunch, clasped by a
papery sheath where they are attached to twig. Number
of needles per bunch is 2, 3, or 5 depending on the sort of
pine it is.

Spruce: Short, stiff needles, angular in cross-section like
a shoemaker's awl, set singly, not in bunches, around a
twig. Each needle is attached to a curved peg. Sure sign
of spruce is to remove needle and see its peg fixed to

twig. Also note roughness of the older twigs with pegs left where needles fell. You can tell spruce in the dark simply by feeling twig.

Hemlock: Short, flat needles in horizontal plane along twig. Undersides have two white lines. Note tiny upside-down needles lying along top of twig between outspreading rows of needles.

Fir: Short, flat needles like hemlock, but longer, lighter green. When needle is removed, no projection is left on twig as with spruce; instead a smooth round mark with dot in center. Another point is that cones stand up on fir, while on other evergreens they usually turn down.

Larch: Short flexible needles spout from ends of heavy spurs on branch. Needles are cast off in winter leaving twigs bare, and spurs give branches lumpy, coarse appearance.

Cedar: Two kinds of needles spell red cedar. Some are tightly fitting, overlapping scales that do not stick out but fit tightly around twig, and others are short, sharp needles that flare haphazardly. White cedar has only one kind of needle: smooth, rounded overlapping scales that make the twig light green, polished, decorative.

Pine needles grow in clusters.   Spruce needles are on tiny pegs.   Fir needles leave small circle with dot in it.

THE PINES

★★White Pine is the rugged, giant pine tree of northeast United States. You often see it as a solitary, massive survivor of white pine forests that have vanished into lumber. Heavy limbs stab out at right angles from the trunk. The angular dark masses of foliage show bright light of sky between. Twigs tend to grow upward above their branches so that the needle masses are underscored by horizontal black line of limb on which they grow. The general effect of an old white pine is that of a broad, eccentric triangle.

On the ground under a white pine you'll find artistic cones, some up to six inches long. These are gracefully curved. Their plates are wide open, showing how the seeds have been discharged. These hard, tough cones make a crackling, cheery fire, with bright bursts from the incandescent resin with which they are heavily sugared. White pine cones with tassels of needles are the State Flower of Maine. This pine cone makes an attractive indoor decoration. Cones on the ground fell after their seeds were gone. Overhead in the branches, mostly near the top of the tree, grow younger cones, with their ripening seeds sealed in tightly beneath smooth green plates.

Note the way pine needles grow in bunches. Count them. White pine has 5 needles clasped together. They have the feel of flexible, springy wires 4 inches long. Straight rows of tiny white dots are the breathing pores of the needle. Peer closely and see how the edges are

**Cone of
White Pine**

saw-toothed. Such perfection of details reveals the precision that goes into the making of a tree.

White pine branches spring out in whorls around the trunk at the rate of one whorl a year. You can tell the age of a white pine by counting these whorls from base to top. Add three for the first years when the seedling did not produce regular side branches. This age token is inaccurate for old specimens when bark has obliterated the marks left by whorls of early years.

White pine has vitality. The seeds from a single tree can people an undisturbed meadow with young white pines in a year or two. Youthful pines may grow 4 feet in height and an inch in diameter in one year.

The tree is named after the clean, white wood. This was the timber of the tall masts and spars of New England clipper ships. Pine panels, fragrant with age, are a prize feature of colonial houses. Widths of upwards of 3 feet testify to the size of trees in the vanished white pine forests of New England.   *Pinus strobus*

Red Pine (also called Norway pine) is the other big, valuable pine tree. It is more northerly than white pine.

Red Pine cone

Wood is as good, and is usually sold as white pine. Red pine is tall and straight with red bark. Healthy, grows fast, is excellent for reforestation. Be on lookout for one of best pines of our Northeast. Needles are extra long, clasped together in 2's.   *Pinus resinosa*

Pitch Pine is the small pine tree you encounter in large numbers along New England's coast. In New Jersey pitch pine covers hundreds of sandy square miles, make an unusual and famous type of forest known as the New Jersey pine barrens. This is also the pine of rocky hilltops where it invites your camera for a windblown picture. Cones hang on after discharg-

Pitch Pine cone

ing seeds; they are dynamic, broad, wide open, add much to the artistry of the branches. You can't miss this tree— needles (in 3's) are sharp, stiff; stand out at right angles. It's a fighter. *Pinus rigida*

Scotch Pine is a bent, leaning tree often planted in poor, dry soil. Perhaps seen more often than others by city people, as it has been much used for gravelly spots in parks, and in large numbers around

Scotch Pine cone

reservoirs. Foliage is light-colored with needles in 2's. You can call out the name of Scotch pine when you see orange bark, especially bright orange toward upper part of trunk and on branches. *Pinus sylvestris*

Jack Pine has shortest needles in 2's. They twist and separate with a flare that gives tree light, airy aspect. Cones are small, narrow, hard; they are curved, hug the bark tightly closed. Like the counterpart of this tree, lodgepole pine

Jack Pine cone

of the far West, it takes a fire to crack cones open and discharge seeds. Jack pine is most northern of the eastern pines. Common around Great Lakes, in dry sandy places.   *Pinus banksiana*

Scrub Pine has 2 short needles that stick out at angles. Looks like jack pine. Makes broad, picturesque, scrubby patches in southern New Jersey and Virginia.   *Pinus virginiana*

Scrub Pine cone

THE SPRUCES

Norway Spruce points skyward, high and sharp as a church steeple. Bottom branches, instead of dropping off like most spruces, sweep out close to ground with a low curve, giving a broad formal base to a towering tent. You always see it beside square Victorian houses, in cemeteries, older parks, on University campuses such as University of Vermont, Burlington. Easy to recognize by its twigs that dangle on older trees instead of poking out stiffly. Bears longest of spruce cones. Look for these handsome ovals; rhythmic, with lights and shadows spiralling across the evenly spaced surfaces of their many scales. This big spruce is an out-of-date tree from the lace curtain era.   *Picea abies*

Norway
Spruce cone

Blue Spruce is styled for decoration. Stiff branches are horizontal. Bottom branches hold on vigorously, making a healthy, dense pyramid that conceals its own trunk. You know it by the light, gray-blue color of needles. Blue spruce is native in Colorado where it acquired the ability to grow in a dry place. Next to Norway, it is the most commonly planted spruce in eastern states, a staple of the nursery industry. See also page 179.   *Picea pungens*

Three spruces are left to know: red, white and black. They all look alike, compact, acute arrow heads pointing skyward from the mountains and bogs up north. They are the trees of places least disturbed by man until recently. Dark and timeless spruce settles in cold north woods humus to create the wilderness home of beaver, bear, and deer. Spruce is constructed to hold deep, white burdens of snow on its stiff branches. Their quivering wood is so resonant it makes sounding boards for violin and piano. Today more and more people are seeing spruce, as these are the trees of the land of the skiers. But spruce forests have been invaded in another way. The streams of northern United States and Canada carry not only the canoes of fishermen and hunters but some are jammed with logs crunching and jerking their way to the pulp mill, to turn up at your newsstand. It takes the annual growth of a stand of 252 acres of spruce forest for an average Sunday edition of the New York Daily News. Paper companies are developing forest management to protect the supply of this valuable tree.

Red Spruce is the spruce tree seen all over the Adirondacks, Green and White Mountains. It is the spruce of Bear Mountain, highest mountain in Connecticut, and

Greylock, highest in Massachusetts. Red spruce fronts
the ocean on the Maine coast, looks picturesque through
the spray above the rocks. Look for the small red cones.
These lovely, broad ovals lie on the ground under the
tree which sheds them every year. The amber gum oozing
from the trunk is good chewing.   *Picea rubra*

White Spruce is the tall lumber of the north woods. Its
needles have a whitish tint which labels the tree from a
distance, gives it the name. White is taller, with longer
cones than other spruces. Cones are cylindrical, smooth,
tan-colored, about two inches long. Resin on trunk and
branches turns white when it dries. Superb and valuable
as it is, white spruce is identified by the bad odor of its
young twigs and needles. Crush them and take a whiff.
This is the chief tree of the Canadian forest, and supplies
most of the pulp for newsprint.   *Picea glauca*

Black Spruce is the courageous, rugged tree for your
drawing pad. It makes a sharp arrow head when young,
but top becomes tortured by its struggle with the severe
climate of the cold northern bog where it grows. Dwarfed

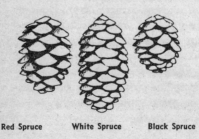

Red Spruce   White Spruce   Black Spruce

by subzero temperatures, black spruce only a few feet high may be 50 years old. This is the tree of the famous floating bogs of northern Minnesota. Sometimes a lower branch reaching out and down penetrates the sphagnum mosses and takes root. Older black spruce is loaded with countless little purple cones that hang on for years. Next to white spruce, this is Canada's most important source of paper pulp.   *Picea mariana*

HEMLOCK

Hemlock is music in the form of a tree. It is a tall, graceful spiral like a Christmas card evergreen, but with sweeping, curved lines, instead of the stiff staccato of spruce. Hemlock needles are flattened and rounded at the tips while spruce are 4-angled and sharp. The top surface of hemlock needle is polished and curved, reflecting blue highlights of the sky that shimmer through its foliage. Such trilling blue light is peculiar to this tree— don't miss seeing it. Little red-brown cones dangle from the tips of flexible wiry twigs, vibrating up and down.

Needles are attached spirally around their twig, but their stalks bend so as to hold them in a horizontal plane forming two rows on each side of twig. Underside of needle has two white lines, and a sure token of hemlock is the row of upside- down needles flat along upper side of twig.

This is one of the decorative trees of our woods. Growing farther south, or lower on mountain sides, than spruce and fir, you see it often mingling with

Hemlock cone

maple, beech, elm, and hickory. Its place must be damp, and hemlock is at its best in shadowy ravines. New York Botanical Garden has fine old hemlock grove.

Hemlock wood is second-rate which may be why we can still see many of these stately and beautiful trees. It splinters, warps, is filled with knots as hard as rocks, and makes dangerous firewood that throws out sparks.

Tsuga canadensis

BALSAM FIR

Balsam Fir holds title as the north woods' most popular tree, with delicious fragrance released by the needles after they dry. Confusion between kinds of evergreens reaches a climax when balsam fir pillows are labeled a breath from the "pines." Because needles are fragrant and hang on longer in the house, this is better Christmas tree than spruce. When you buy, test for fir by removing a needle, see if twig is left smooth with tiny round mark and dot in its center. (This test does not apply to Douglas fir, the leading Christmas tree out west.) Needles are

flat with whitish underside; longer, lighter green than spruce and hemlock.

Balsam fir bark has little blisters containing clear reservoirs of resin. This is so pure it is used for cementing microscope lenses and mounting microscopic specimens. Every laboratory worker knows "Canada balsam."

Balsam Fir cone stands upright on twig.

Cones stand erect like candles on

fir tree boughs. On other evergreens they dangle or are turned down. The big cylinders three inches long and an inch thick look too heavy for the twigs. However, every camper who has made his bed with springy balsam boughs knows how easily and gaily they carry weight.

Abies balsamea

LARCH

Larch (also called tamarack) sheds its needles in the fall, and grows a complete set of fresh needles in the spring like a broadleaf tree. Yet, when needles are out, larch looks like any normal evergreen and bears small, tan cones resembling hemlock's. This extraordinary behavior of a cone-bearing tree is also a feature of bald cypress. Both larch and bald cypress grow in swamps, and it is interesting to speculate whether roots in water may have influenced these two cone-bearing trees to become leaf droppers.

Another claim to fame is the appearance of larch in its far north bogs—always straight, clean, serene, while its companions, black spruce and balsam fir, are usually wind-twisted, look like fierce fighters of the elements. These three trees grow northward to the treeline tundra above the Arctic Circle.

Needles, like seasonal leaves, are soft, moist, compared to the crisp, woody needles on other cone-bearing trees. They are less than an inch long, and radiate from the tips of wooden knobs, a bunch of some 18 spraying out at wide angles. They are blue-

Larch cones

green; foliage is feathery and light-tinted. New twigs of
the season, before woody knobs are formed, put forth
needles scattered along singly. One feature not so easily
seen is the system of long, tough root fibers that may
drop twenty feet through a bog to get a firm bottom.
These root strings are as heavy as waxed thread used
by a shoemaker. Indians used them to sew together birch
bark canoes.   *Larix laricina*

THE CEDARS

Entirely different in style from all other trees of our
landscape, cedars can be instantly recognized. Among
trees that are tall, loose, and reaching, cedar looks clipped
formal, geometric. Foliage is compact and dark. Density
is increased by myriads of tiny twigs concealed by overlapping needles so that a cedar may appear as having no
branches, but built out of a mass of green shaped into a
pyramid or oval.

Three kinds of cedar of eastern states are easily recognized with a little practice. But you seldom see all three
growing near each other. The different cedars herd together in different places, and the first way to identify
one is by the place where you see it.

Red Cedar peppers New England hillsides like an exclamation point turned upside down. In South and Middle West red cedar takes a wider, explosive form. Leaves
are scales so small you can barely see them with naked
eye; but look closely and admire how perfectly they overlap and cover twig on four sides, making twig appear
square in cross-section. Young twigs have needles sharp

and long, entirely different from the
scale needles. Best check on red cedar is
the small, sky blue berries. These are
"cones" whose scales have turned waxy
and blue and become welded together.
Heartwood is beautiful red with aroma
fragrant to our nostrils but hated by
moths. This is the wood for lining closets
and cedar chests.   *Juniperus virginiana*

Red Cedar has two
kinds of needles.

Arbor Vitae (also called northern white cedar) is the
marvelous yellow-green column in the coldest parts of
New England and Lake states. You can
plant cuttings of fresh twigs in sand and
grow them easily for planting around
your home. Nurserymen offer tailor-made
specimens. Twig is covered by overlapping scales as tightly fitting as a snake's
skin. Branching twigs form flat, polished frond, one of the most artistic designs discovered on the twigs of any tree
in the world. Wood resists decay, makes good shingles
and fence posts.   *Thuja occidentalis*

Arbor
Vitae

Southern White Cedar is a dark swamp
tree that hugs the Atlantic coast. This is
the tree of the cedar bogs, feature of the
famous New Jersey pine barrens. Trunks
buried in New Jersey swamp mud were
dredged up, untouched by rot, turned
into tough PT boats in Second World
War. Resonant wood makes good pipe
organs.   *Chamaecyparis thyoides*

Southern
White Cedar

THE MIDDLE WEST_____

Trees pour into the Middle West from four points of the compass, so people there cannot boast of many of their own kinds of trees. Trees seen in New England cross the Appalachians, spread out over most of the Middle West. Everywhere are big standard trees—elm, white oak, hickory, trembling aspen, sycamore, beech, tulip, willow, maple, cherry, and the understory witch hazel, sassafras, hop hornbeam.

Nevertheless, the mixing in of southern and prairie trees, the dropping out of northern ones like paper birch, changes the emphasis, gives Middle West trees a distinctive aspect. Many more black walnut, sweetgum, hackberry, persimmon, hawthorn, honey locust appear on every hand. Black cherry grows larger. Shagbark hickory becomes shellbark. Sugar maple is called hard or rock maple. White and gray birch disappear, and abundant river birches line the waterways. Cottonwood joins with trembling aspen. Bur oak becomes the Middle West's greatest oak, abundant in Kansas and Nebraska. This is a true Middle West tree. It contests possession of land with prairie grasses, pushing forest fingers into the wide open spaces. These groves with no understory of trees or shrubs, but with carpets of clean grass are famous as "bur oak openings."

Between the Corn Belt of Kansas and Iowa and the Appalachians are nine states that form a huge mixing bowl of trees. This holds the greatest number of species and the most broadleaf trees of any forest of America. The northern part of this tree domain has millions of acres of evergreens. Indeed, white pine, which was the backbone of New England's shipbuilding a century ago, today has its best stands in Minnesota, Wisconsin, and Michigan.

Most of the original forest has been replaced by farmland, but from the Tennessee mountains and from farm woodlands we get a large quantity of the best-grade hardwood lumber.

The Middle West might well claim to be headquarters of the Great American Woods. People traveling back and forth between the nine states of the central forest and eastern states meet no great surprises nor puzzling styles of trees as they would when traveling south or far west. The Appalachians oppose no barrier to interchanging our best-known trees. Certain trees that are especially characteristic of the Middle West are as follows:

★**Bur Oak** (also called mossycup oak) is king of the White Oak Group in the Middle West. Its massive black trunk and big horizontal limbs make impressive silhouette in the murk around Chicago. Patriarchal aspect is heightened by deep furrowed

Bur Oak Acorn

bark. This is so fire-resistant that it explains the survival of many giant bur oaks, especially in woods of Indiana and Illinois. Westward where wooded country shades off to prairie, bur oak forms open groves, contesting the land with the grasses. Small bur oaks bridge the Great Plains and turn up in the foothills of the Rockies. Two peculiar details tell the bur oak: leaf is almost cut in two where the opposite sinuses try to meet. Acorn cup is extra deep, covering half the nut, and it is shaggy, with heavy spines on rim.

Bur Oak

Quercus macrocarpa

★**Box Elder** (also called ash-leaved maple) is the tree you see everywhere in the Middle West. Double-winged seeds always tag a maple—just as acorns always identify an oak. Box elder's winged seeds make a sharp angle like closing scissors. They hang on most of the winter. Leaf is multiple with 3-leaflets (sometimes 5)—the only maple with an un-maple-like leaf. But the over-all outline of 3 leaflets together suggests maple leaf form. Perhaps this

is a diagram of evolution going on before our eyes showing how a standard maple leaf can evolve from 3 leaflets.

Twigs are pastel red, purple, or bright green coated with soft white bloom. Coating rubs off with finger, revealing a glossy twig, and giving inner satisfaction as does rubbing off silver polish to see the shine.

Box Elder leaf is only a step away from conventional Maple leaf.

Branches are brittle, scattered over ground by wind. But tree is planted far and wide along streets. You see it in Chicago, Denver, and Dallas. It's America's most agreeable tree, doing well in high or low places, sunlight or shade, moist or dry places. East of the Alleghanies you seldom see it, and people

Box Elder seeds

from New England might take the leaves for poison ivy. It branches out this way and that spontaneously with no clear shape. Wood is soft and used to make cheap furniture, easily broken toys. *Acer negundo*

Osage Orange was an industry before the invention of barbed wire. Western settlers used it for fencing to keep out cattle. Touching it carelessly gives you shock from 1-inch thorns sharp as needles. Remnants of old hedges remain with "oranges" hanging among barby branches or rolling down onto the road where they often squash and make mess with seeds and pulp. This peculiar fruit on the ground signals to passerby that osage orange is near. It is like a big green orange, but stippling is coarser, its rounded bumps and ridges vaguely suggesting a brain. Milky sap from fruit and broken twigs has pungent fragrance of oriental lacquer, sticks to hands, quickly turns black. Fruit is inedible, but small boys use it to play catch.

This healthy, dangerous tree has wonderful wood. Heartwood is yellow streaked with red, enclosed in white sapwood, and takes a luxurious polish. Elastic, so Indians made bows of it; and we make policemen's clubs.

Osage Orange

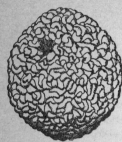

Fruit of Osage Orange

Leaves are smooth, curly and gay—catching highlights in a striking way. Bark is yellow (bark on roots is surprisingly bright orange), and deeply furrowed like black locust.

Osage orange is a museum piece from the settlement of our western prairies. First settlers in St. Louis got it from Oklahoma and Texas Indians; later, men profited by selling osage orange for use as barbed wire fences that need no repairing, came rigged up with fence posts. *Maclura pomifera*

Sorrel Tree (also called sour wood) is the mystery tree of the hills from Ohio southward. It peppers the woods where oak, maple, hickory, and such well-known trees grow. The tree is inconspicuous, middle-sized. Bark is nondescript like sour gum; leaf is unexciting, glossy, oval like peach tree. Nobody notices sorrel tree until something happens.

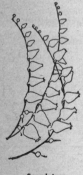

Sorrel tree flowers

The first event occurs in mid-summer when other tree flowers are gone and forgotten. Then this straight, clean tree holds out clusters of thousands of white flowers like lilies-of-the-valley. They dangle in rows on curving stems 7 inches long. Each flower is an exquisite white bell. These are fragrant, and a source of good honey, making one of the world's best bee trees. Each flower turns into a seedcase, a gray urn shaped like the white

flower, that is a remarkable bit of tree jewelry. The second event is the fall color of
sorrel tree. Leaves are sour, taste one, as
this is a point of identification; the lemony
tang is pleasant. Acid in the sap turns leaves
bright red when frostbitten. The pinky red
of sorrel tree is one of the fine sights of the
woods around Chattanooga and southward.
Its foliage can compete with sugar maple
on this score.   *Oxydendrum arboreum*

Sorrel tree

Kentucky Coffee Tree shows how eccentric a tree can
be. Branches are bare until late in spring; leaves fall before all others. Translation of its scientific name "Gymnocladus" describes it well; first part means "naked," as in
gymnasium where you strip for exercise, and "cladus"
means branch. The twigs are fat, crooked and appear
coated with old whitewash that has turned gray and is
flaking off. See the colorful, salmon-pink pith in their
center.

Double multiple leaves (compare honey
locust and Hercules'-club) are enormous,
up to 3 feet long. These appear magically
out of tiny winter buds that are almost in-
visible. Leaves are so open they cast little
shade, but filter the sunlight. Big broad pods
seem made of tough old leather, dark red,
blackened with age. Half a dozen hard
seeds rattle in these pods. First settlers in
Kentucky, cut off from coffee, ground up
these seeds, made a good substitute. They
thought their coffee tree was a wonderful

Seed-pod of
Kentucky
Coffee tree

discovery that would make them rich, but imported coffee won out. Eccentric twigs and big leaves make a picturesque lawn tree. Planted as such especially in South Dakota.   *Gymnocladus dioica*

Kentucky Coffee tree

"We think the typical American trees and flowers are those described in our own tree and flower guides —elm, oak, maple; witch hazel, sassafras, shadblow; alder, blueberry, hazelnut; violet, marsh marigold, iris—these are typical big trees, little trees, shrubs, and flowers of our hardwood forest. These are as American as baseball. Yet they did not always grow here. They were not even created on our hills and valleys. They came from the south, where they fled from the Big Ice and then radiated north over the glacial delta. They were returning to where they had been before the Ice came. While this part of the continent was being rebuilt by the Big Ice, our American forest was crowded down along the slopes of the southern Alleghenies."

from OUR FLOWERING WORLD

Wafer Ash (also called hop tree) hangs beautiful bunches of circles all over itself. Each circle resembles modern plastic. It has two seeds in a compressed box surrounded by a translucent creamy-green diaphragm an inch across. These exquisite circles show how nature has been way ahead of us in creating plastics, efficiently, simply, out of sap and sunshine.

Smooth-edged leaves in multiples of 3 leaflets, shiny, could be mistaken for poison ivy. Wafer ash grows on edges of woods in shade, especially on rocky slopes in the Mississippi valley. For closer acquaintance, taste and smell the bitter bark.   *Ptelea trifoliata*

Wafer Ash

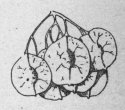

Plastic-like discs of
Wafer Ash

Pawpaw looks tropical. Big 12-inch leaves spout from the tips of upturned branches, and then droop with their weight, making a pattern of green umbrellas. In April triangular flowers bloom, the color of well-done beefsteak. Bees and insects like their odor, but it's disagreeable to us. These dark peculiar flowers are inconspicuous in shadows, but their fruit is famous; a fat, short banana, overripe, with dark brown, loose skins, containing an insipid yellow custard. If we didn't have regular bananas, there might be a market for pawpaw fruit. Seeds look like lima beans. This is northern version of tropical custard apple. Pawpaw grows biggest in southern Indiana and Tennessee near streams flowing into Ohio River. Middle Westerners find it in bottom-land thickets.

Asimina triloba

Wahoo (also called burning bush) is the little tree of Arkansas that has four-lobed, flame-red fruit. In most of the Middle West it's a bush with equally startling fruit in fall. New Englanders match the display with garden shrubs related to this tree or with their climbing bittersweet. Indians made arrows of wood; if you say "wahoo" with vigor, it sounds like an arrow taking off.

Euonymus atropurpureus

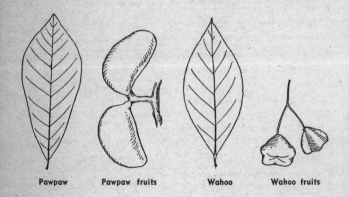

Pawpaw   Pawpaw fruits   Wahoo   Wahoo fruits

THE SOUTH_____

Many trees you see in New England are growing down south: elm, oak, walnut, maple, sycamore, poplar, willow, tulip, locust, dogwood, ash. Even typically northern trees as sugar maple, shagbark hickory, red oak, and basswood have traveled to Alabama on the Appalachian ridges but that doesn't make them southern trees. In reverse, sweet gum, honey locust, hackberry, sassafras move north.

However, as you drive south, it's thrilling to see trees change. Certain kinds have the flavor of the South, and, if you're a northerner, give you the feeling of being away. No one who travels through our south Atlantic and Gulf states should miss southern magnolia, holly, live oak, bald cypress. In addition, hackberry, persimmon, sweet gum, black gum, honey locust are larger and more numerous.

South of Washington, D. C., you drive through mile after mile of tall, straight pines. This is part of the biggest pine forest in the world. It occupies much of the coastal plain, a broad band 100 to 300 miles wide to Florida and then westward around the Gulf of Mexico into Texas. Loblolly, shortleaf, longleaf, and slash (all four called southern yellow pine by lumbermen) are the big four. In the midst of this vast, sandy kingdom are swamps and bayous where grows the only bald cypress in the world.

Not characteristic of our South, but with peculiar interest, the southern part of Florida holds the only subtropical trees in the U. S. A. This is so despite the post card concept of palmetto and moss-draped live oak as being tropical vegetation. They are southern, and picturesque, of course, but not tropical.

If you live in the North, eight oaks of the South are surprising. The first five have plain oval leaves, unlike typical oak leaves. The next three have whimsical leaves to delight your eye.

★★Live Oak is the South's post card tree. It has an ample, easy-going contour, with comfortable horizontal limbs from which silvery Florida moss swings lazily. This festoonery is not a true moss but a queer member of the pineapple family that lives on air, uses trees and telegraph wires for support. You begin to see live oaks on south side of Chesapeake Bay; they follow the coast to Texas, are fine street trees in Savannah, New Orleans, and are features of the famous deep South gardens.

Massive limbs, bigger than most tree trunks, travel far out horizontally—one of the wonders of wood. Your arm straight out cannot support great weight. Consider what strength bears the tonnage of these limbs against the leverage applied where they join their trunk. Wood is even harder than the mighty white oak and was used for shipbuilding until steel took its place.

Leaves are small, smooth-margined ovals, whitish beneath, dark glossy green on top. The notion that trees stripped of leaves in winter are dead gives name to live oak—it has evergreen leaves.

Look for graceful acorns. Slender, one-inch, rich chestnut-brown, tapering at both ends. This landmark of plantations is also common in scrubby form on sand dunes.

Quercus virginiana

Water Oak is seen much along streams, and as a street tree in coastal towns. Leaves oval, but often broader near tip forming pear-shape; hang on until Christmas.

Quercus nigra

Willow Oak is a fine shade tree around southern homes, and is often seen on low hills and near swamps and streams. Leathery, narrow leaves are pointed at both ends.

Quercus phellos

Laurel Oak is tall with glistening, almost evergreen leaves and black bark. A common street tree in Far South towns, a big tree in eastern Florida. Leaves have bristle at tip, stems are yellow with interesting groove.

Quercus laurifolia

Shingle Oak has large shiny oval leaves with wavy margins. Note bowl-shaped acorns. Handsome park tree. Southern mountains and uplands, abundant in Missouri. Wood is fine for clapboards and shingles, hence its name.

Quercus imbricaria

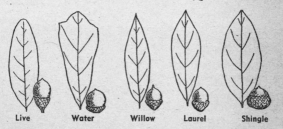

Live   Water   Willow   Laurel   Shingle

When traveling through the South, don't overlook whimsical leaf patterns on the following three oaks:

Spanish Oak has fluid leaves with slender lobes that curve like scimitars. They are utterly gay, freely drawn, a real delight if you have an eye for informal design. This lovely shade tree is common on dry uplands; and often makes acres of woods in sandy soil in Virginia and southward.   *Quercus falcata*

Black Jack Oak is the common, scrubby, crooked oak that decorates poor sandy places all over the South (and as far north as New Jersey). Instead of passing it by for cooler, shadier places, pause and see the leaves. They round out with three lobes at top, have the outline of a boy's kite, or, turned around, they suggest broad bells.
                                             Quercus marilandica

Overcup Oak has a curious leaf with wide lobes at the top, narrow at the bottom, as though leaves from two kinds of oak had been cut in half and fitted together. A large tree beside coastal rivers and in deep swamps. You know it instantly if you find acorns with rough cup that all but encloses and hides the nut part.   *Quercus lyrata*

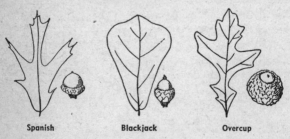

Spanish   Blackjack   Overcup

BALD CYPRESS

★★**Bald Cypress** is as great a feature of the South as live oak. To see only these two trees gives you a lifelong memory of what our South looks like. From Chesapeake Bay southward highways run through swampy areas where standing water shimmers. Unlike scrubby tangle and stunted trees in northern bogs, a stately forest rises out of the water and muck. This is headquarters of bald cypress—the only region in the world where it grows. The farther south you go the more this forest is draped with swaying Florida moss—it all looks and feels like a tropical jungle of awesome stillness, and with cathedral-like twilight. This peculiar soft glow contrasts with the black shadows of northern needle-tree forests. Cypress needles are pale green and wide open in the form of delicate feathers that filter sky brightness, and let diffused light permeate the forest. This is softened again by silvery festoons, and around the tree bases eerie brightness is reflected from mirrors of still water.

Notice the engineering of a bald cypress. The superb trunk tapers gradually from a wide, flaring base, formed like the shoulder of a bottle. This is fluted and buttressed. Thus, the center of gravity is lowered to help balance a tonnage of wood held straight

Fluted trunk and "knees"
of Bald Cypress

and slender a hundred feet into the sky, though anchored in unstable water and mud.

You may see things that look like small stumps, or knots of roots around the base. These are the famous cypress knees. Often they make fantastic shapes—wood sculpturing at its most imaginative. The knee is a unique invention of bald cypress to get more air into the tree's system, prevent drowning of the roots. Ordinary trees get enough air from spaces between soil particles, but steps have to be taken to get more air when tree roots are under still water. Knees are just the right height to hold their tops above the average water level in that place.

Cones are round, an inch across. Strangely, this cone-bearing needle tree drops its needles and also twigs to which they're attached. This makes it look dead, and when fresh, feathery needles come out in the spring, they tint the soft glow of a cypress swamp with iridescent bluish-green.

Cypress wood is almost decay-proof—excellent for gutters, coffins, and shingles.   *Taxodium distichum*

Pond Cypress is a smaller version of bald cypress, seen farther south, along Tamiami Trail and lower Everglades. Needles are pressed along twig instead of stretched out in form of feather.

Taxodium ascendens

Pond Cypress

PALMETTO

★★**Palmetto** captures the imagination as a South Sea Island symbol of Florida's climate. It grows all over Florida, forms dense groves on Everglade hammocks, and palmetto finds pockets of warm sun as far north as South Carolina. You know it from other palms because its leaves are huge fans that stick out like pins in a pincushion ball at the top of the trunk. This is the leaf much used by churches on Palm Sunday. Palmetto is all trunk and leaves, no branches. The trunk is heavy, equal in diameter all the way up. Often it is enclosed in a loose basket made by the crisscross of old leaf stems. Sometimes leaves, instead of falling off, turn down and form a straw skirt. The fibers of leaf stems are used to make whisk brooms. Older palmettos have smooth gray trunks like cement. It's almost as durable; therefore palmetto trunks make good piling for wharves.

On the trunk top sits a single huge bud, the size and style of an artichoke. This is delicious to eat when cooked like a cabbage. (Local people call the tree cabbage palm.) But the removal of the bud ends the tree's life, and who would destroy fifty years of tree building for a single dish?

Just look at the palmetto and consider that this tree, with nothing about it such as wood, bark, bud, or leaf like ordinary trees, is from the Age of Reptiles.

Palmetto leaf

Sabal palmetto

PERSIMMON

Persimmon is the possum tree. The furry little animal gorges himself on the fruit, falls asleep hanging by his tail. Lacking the possum, there are other ways of recognizing persimmon.

This is mostly a southern tree, common in the woods, but left in fields and along roads by people who cleared the forest because they liked its fruit—and also wanted to catch possum. Thus you'll see plenty of persimmon when driving through, for example, North Carolina.

Persimmon arrests the eye, especially with leaves off. You'll say, "What are those trees with the crooked branches?" The trunk is graceful and straight, but the branches spring out above like mad snakes.

In the fall, after the leaves have dropped, the persimmon fruits look like little, tired, yellow apples; but when they look the most spoiled and wrinkled, they taste their best. An unripe persimmon is filled with tannic acid, a powerful astringent. If eaten then, it shrivels your mouth painfully so that you'd rather be stung by a wasp. This tree is a member of the Ebony Family, the hard, black wood from tropical jungles. Persimmon wood is only streaked with black. Harder than oak, it is used for spinning shuttles and for wooden golf club heads.

Possum in
Persimmon tree.
Notice chunky
bark.

Diospyros virginiana

THE GUM TREES_____

★Sweet Gum rewards you with more peculiar surprises than any other tree of our land. Leaves offer instant identification—clear, well-made stars, the size of maple leaves. Five points are spaced as a six-pointed star, one omitted where the stem is attached. These star-leaves have a high gloss, making the whole tree twinkle in the sun. If you have a sweet gum near your home, make a note to look at it in the rain, for when wet, leaves are stars of glass with silver dripping from their points. As for fall color, no note is needed, for the deep wine-red of these leaves will stop you with their beauty.

Leaves and buds of sweet gum crushed between your fingers have a woodsy, resin odor. The deep, corky bark oozes with chewy sweet resin gum— also fragrant, one of the real natural perfumes, simply waiting to be enjoyed. It offers good chewing gum for the taking. Drug manufacturers make tincture of benzoin of it.

Sweet Gum

Through the mid-South this is one of the commonest large trees

Thorny ball of
Sweet Gum

seen. This clean, straight tree is often used as a shade tree in many towns of the Ohio River Valley; for example, Cincinnati and Louisville. People who walk along streets with their noses down will see one-inch thorny balls on the ground where their shoes crunch them, balls so hard they lie around all winter, and they are tough on auto tires. These peculiar castoff balls, the shells of sweet gum fruits, tag the tree for many people.

Less conspicuous, because they are often high on the tree, are the twigs which bear another surprise. Cork is manufactured at a high rate on them. The bark-making mechanism with an abundance of the fragrant gum ingredient seems to overproduce along the twigs where only a thin bark would be needed. This results in eccentric corky ridges being built up. Cork on twigs is one of the best tags of a sweet gum in winter.

Sweet gum is a leading furniture wood, and, next to black walnut, the greatest for veneers—not in its own

Corky ridges of
Sweet Gum

name but as an imitator! The fine grain has no character of its own but stains to look not only like walnut, but mahogany, maple, or birch. Your television and radio cabinets may be sweet gum.

Danbury, Connecticut, has the farthest north sweet gum, but it is not common north of New Jersey except as street or park trees. Let the scientific name roll off your tongue: "Liquidambar"—a perfect name for a tree that oozes golden balsam. *Liquidambar styraciflua*

*Black Gum (also called sour gum and tupelo) is a sudden exclamation with its short, crooked branches that stab out horizontally from a straight, sharp trunk that is continuous from base to top. Lower branches may slant downward, but the main effect is nearly horizontal. Black gum's zig-zag branch holds leaves, clustered near the end, in a flat mosaic. Each leaf is a smooth oval with no teeth or lobes. Although the simple oval might seem conventional as a leaf form, actually so many trees have compounded their leaves or conjured up fanciful geometric designs that plain oval leaves on trees in the woods and fields of northeastern United States are rare, except on black gum and dogwood. The South, however, has many trees with smooth, oval leaves. The black gum leaf is thickened around the margin, as though it had a rim to give it strength and finish.

This tree exclamation point is more vivid in fall, when the leaves turn intense, deep red. Black gum is one of four medium-sized trees that turn so marvelously rich red that people who are not thinking about individual trees at all are stopped in their tracks; these are black gum, sweet gum, sassafras, and dogwood.

In the South black gum grows to greater size, and is common, often found in damp ground with red maple. Occasionally an old black gum in an open field in the mid-South develops with heavy, widely reaching limbs that remind a traveler from New England of white oak until he looks at the leaves.

Nyssa sylvatica

Black Gum

Water Tupelo, another gum of the South, grows in swamps with bald cypress. Like black gum in most ways, it distinguishes itself by standing in water and unstable muck, and has a remarkable, swollen base to give it a low center of gravity and keep it from toppling over.

The wood of both black gum and tupelo is peculiar in the way it is reinforced with tough, crooked fibres that interlock the grain. This makes it hard to split—fine for hubs, wooden wheels on roller skates, rollers for wire cables to pull coal cars in anthracite mines.

Nyssa biflora

**Bulging base helps Water
Tupelo stand upright in
unstable muck.**

Sugar maple, a distinctly American tree, is a masterpiece of art in every detail. (Hotchkiss School, Lakeville, Conn.)

Massive arching branches of live oaks, festooned with Florida moss, give picturesque atmosphere to the deep South.

Pitch pine is picturesque tree of rocky and sandy places. (Photograph shows Connecticut's highest tree, atop Bear Mt.)

A native Washington palm towers above lush planting at Sequoia High School, Redwood City, California.

Ponderosa pine is the tree feature of the scenery of Rocky Mountain National Park, near Denver, Colo.

Branch pattern of white oak vibrates with its strength and vitality.

Sweet gum quietly opens its leaf stars on the rim of the tragic Crater at Petersburg, Va.

Underwater roots of bald cypress breathe through their peculiar knees. This tree of our South is unique in all the world.

Just before leaves cast shade, the Great American woods gets a brilliant carpet of spring flowers.

LEFT: Peeling paper birch.   RIGHT: Silvery gray birch.

LEFT: Thorny honey locust. (Morton Arboretum, Lisle, Ill.)
RIGHT: Satiny cherry. (Brooklyn Botanic Garden)